Living with Dogs

A commonsense guide

Living with Dogs

A commonsense guide

Dr Hugh Wirth

ABC Books

 The ABC 'Wave' device is a trademark of the Australian Broadcasting Corporation and is used under licence by HarperCollins*Publishers* Australia.

First published in Australia in 1995 by Lothian Books, Melbourne
This revised edition published by HarperCollins*Publishers* Australia Pty Limited
ABN 36 009 913 517
harpercollins.com.au

Copyright © Dr Hugh Wirth and the Estate of Richard Yallop 2010

The right of Dr Hugh Wirth and Richard Yallop to be identified
as the authors of this work has been asserted under
the *Copyright Amendment (Moral Rights) Act 2000*.

This work is copyright. Apart from any use as permitted under the
Copyright Act 1968, no part may be reproduced, copied, scanned,
stored in a retrieval system, recorded, or transmitted, in any form
or by any means, without the prior written permission of the publisher.

HarperCollins*Publishers*
25 Ryde Road, Pymble, Sydney, NSW 2073, Australia
31 View Road, Glenfield, Auckland 0627, New Zealand
A 53, Sector 57, Noida, UP, India
77–85 Fulham Palace Road, London W6 8JB, United Kingdom
2 Bloor Street East, 20th floor, Toronto, Ontario M4W 1A8, Canada
10 East 53rd Street, New York NY 10022, USA

National Library of Australia Cataloguing-in-Publication data:

Wirth, Hugh, 1939-
    Living with dogs / Hugh Wirth.
    2nd ed.
    ISBN: 978 0 7333 2888 6 (pbk.)
    Dogs – Behavior.
    Dogs – Health.
    Other Authors/Contributors: Australian Broadcasting Corporation.
636.7

Cover and internal design by Priscilla Nielsen
Cover images by shutterstock.com
Typeset in Sabon 11/15pt by Letter Spaced

CONTENTS

Introduction	1
Part 1. Your new dog	17
Selecting your perfect partner	19
Breeds	35
The puppy comes home	59
Part 2. Behaviour	75
Boss dogs and behaviour problems	77
Happy dogs	93
Contented owners	109
Part 3. Health	123
Getting rid of pests	125
A case for the vet	138
Part 4. Dogs in the community	153
The fight for dogs' rights	155
When the law bites	173
Part 5. Your dog problems	183
New dog	186
Behaviour	192
Health	206
Older dogs	216
Dogs and children	218
Emergencies	219
Services for your dog	222
RSPCA addresses	225
Index	228

INTRODUCTION

Best of Mates

From earliest childhood I was determined to get a dog. My father had bred and shown English Setters, and my mother came from a traditional family that had a dog and a cat. When I was born in 1939, my parents had a Scottish Terrier called Angus, but when I was only two years old he had to be put down because he suffered from severe dermatitis, and the vets then didn't have the same armoury of medicines we now have to treat dogs with skin problems. There had only been time for Angus to make the briefest impression on me, but it was enough to spark a lifetime's attachment to terriers.

I began to put pressure on my parents to buy me a dog from the time I was five. The answer was always, 'Yes, dear, you can have a dog one day,' but nothing ever happened. That didn't stop me hounding them.

At school I had been entranced by Lessons 6 and 7 in the *First Book of the Victorian Readers*, which featured a dog called Spot. My father worked in the T & G Building in Collins Street, Melbourne, where he made dental appliances. One day when I went to see him in the office, I passed by the window of a pet shop just down the road and saw some black-and-white Fox Terrier puppies who looked just like Spot. From that moment I didn't just want a dog: I wanted a Fox Terrier.

We lived in the suburb of East Ivanhoe, close to the Yarra river. My father was a retiring man who loved his home, and he considered that his role in life was to support the family. My mother was the more dominant and strong-willed. I was the first child and my brother, David, was born three years later. Then there was a gap of 18 months before my second brother, Paul, arrived. My sisters, Elizabeth and Rosemary, completed the family unit, but sadly Elizabeth died when I was 15. The fact that I was on my own so much as a child was one of the reasons I wanted a dog, for the company.

I spent 18 months harping on and on about getting a dog until eventually my father relented and bought a Fox Terrier pup from a breeder. Of course I called him Spot, and I was thrilled to bits because he was my dog.

He was highly spirited and not at all well-mannered. The best thing about him was that he was very energetic, yipping and roaring round and round. With three young boys and Spot racing about, the place was chaotic. My father had always owned setters, which were more sedate, and he never really approved of me having a hyperactive terrier.

Spot and I had an alliance. If I felt my parents had treated me harshly or things were going badly at school, I would confide in Spot and everything would start to seem better. I used to go off and discuss things with him. We would spend hours scampering around the local primary school, and walking along the river. If I got a belting on the backside from my parents, Spot was the only friend I could turn to for consolation. Even then I'd started to realise that when things went badly you could talk to the dog and he'd understand. I've always been a loner, perfectly content with just me and a dog. In my upbringing, the stability factors were the house, my parents and the dog.

I still talk to my dogs. Driving in the car to the supermarket, I tell them things I'd never say to some human beings. I swear they know my moods and they always seem sympathetic. If I'm upset, they're more solicitous to me. If I'm happy, they're happy too. If I'm in a grump, they're not right either.

You can always trust dogs; you never quite know with people. Once they've bonded with you, dogs never let you down. Human beings never tell you everything, but dogs are open; they never hide anything or connive. They build you up because they always think you're great. Who else wags their tail when you come home?

When I'd had Spot for two or three years, I came home from school one day to find that he was missing. My father said he had been stolen by the swaggies who lived down by the river. I never saw Spot again. Being a child, I didn't question what my father said about the swaggies stealing Spot, but ever since then I've wondered exactly what happened to the dog, and whether my parents sent him away because he was such a handful. At the time I was inconsolable. All along I'd felt this overwhelming resistance from my parents to getting the animal I wanted.

Finally, after all the struggle, I had been allowed a dog, and he had become my closest companion. Then, out of the blue, he disappeared. Part of the grief was having to go through all of this again. It had taken me so long to get Spot, and how was I going to persuade my parents to get another dog?

My father replaced Spot with an English Setter called Rajah, a massive disappointment because he had none of the breed characteristics of a Fox Terrier. I've no doubt my father persuaded me to get an English Setter because he thought it would be a calmer family dog than Spot. In modern parlance, Rajah was a wimp. He never wanted to play the roughhouse games I liked. He died from bowel disease when he was young, and within days we had bought an Irish Setter pup called Rufus.

Rufus was everything a young boy could want of a dog. He was involved in everything I ever did. My parents had built a holiday house at Mount Martha and whether we were on the beach, mucking around in the pine plantation, riding bikes or driving round Mount Martha in the Austin Seven, Rufus was always there. He was extremely tolerant, and he would put up with anything. He even allowed himself to be half-buried in the sand. When I had tiffs with my parents, I turned to Rufus.

I'd always had a liking for all animals and when I went from convent school to Xavier College in Kew, I was quite certain, to the point of stubbornness, that I wanted to do veterinary science. A psychologist would probably say, 'Wirth can't get on with humans, so he gets on with animals.' Apart from the dogs, I also had an interest in a

Jersey cow at my convent school in Heidelberg. If I got to school early enough, I would milk it. In those days, after the war, people used to roll up at school in pony carts, because petrol rationing was still in operation, and horses, which still played an important role in society, used to be shod at the old Heidelberg forge, just down the road from the school.

The first public conflict at Xavier about me becoming a vet blew up when I was doing matriculation in 1956. It was the first of many clashes with the establishment that I have since had in my life. Xavier was one of the top private schools in Melbourne, and it was felt that only three occupations were acceptable: the first was the priesthood, the second medicine and the third law. There was a pious hope that if you were going to spread Roman Catholic values in the community, medicine and law were the best ways to do it.

I was told by the master-in-charge of studies that if I had the brains to do veterinary science, I'd have greater impact on the world by doing medicine. There was continual pressure to make me see eye-to-eye with him. I was told I was prostituting myself by going into veterinary science: why fiddle with cows when you can fix humans? The headmaster and I also had a very serious collision over his belief that I was not doing my studies well enough.

My parents always knew I wanted to work with animals. My father didn't want me to be a veterinary surgeon, and clearly told me so, but he never stood in my way. His only demand was that I matriculate. My stubbornness came from my mother, and my parents realised there was no point trying to make me change my mind. Nor did the parish priest manage to dissuade me, although he was continually telling me to do medicine. I listened, but nothing that any of them said made any difference. I've always done what I wanted to do, and there was no way I was going to give in to the teachers and clerics.

I was only the fifth Xavier student in a hundred years to do veterinary science. I started at the University of Queensland in 1959. Melbourne didn't have a course at that time, so the choice was either Brisbane or Sydney, and the consensus among Melbourne vets was that Brisbane was the best place to go.

Up to then, the horse had been the king of the domestic animals and it had always figured prominently in the syllabuses of the veterinary schools. But human reliance on the horse was diminishing, and our professor in Brisbane held the view that we had to concentrate on production animals, which meant sheep and cows, and companion animals, which were mainly cats and dogs.

I was very fortunate that I was one of the last group of students trained by people who had actually been in veterinary practice. There was a large practical component to the course, unlike nowadays when the people who teach veterinary science tend to be pure academics. The Professor of Animal Husbandry was an Englishman called Tom Ewer, and he was the first person to get me thinking about animal welfare issues. Battery hen farming was just starting, and Tom Ewer objected strongly to chooks being put in cages. He had great empathy for animals and said that battery farming impeded the free expression of the chickens.

In my second year I was taught by Glen McBride, who lectured on animal genetics though his real interest was animal behaviour, an area which was then in its absolute infancy. Articles used to appear about McBride in the Brisbane newspapers, saying that he thought that dogs and pigs could talk. I recall that he found that dogs made 32 different sounds in the company of each other. I believe dogs have certain alerting mechanisms and different tones of barking, and even though they don't possess an extensive vocabulary like us, they have a limited but adequate number of sounds with which to communicate.

McBride used to get us to study the behaviour of chickens. He would put numbers on their backs and get us to climb stepladders and observe what each of them did. Some of his colleagues dismissed him as a crank, but he had a big impact on the students. My daily veterinary practice still incorporates beliefs that he and Tom Ewer taught me in those first two years. That was when I realised animal behaviour was an extremely important part of my work. If you want to be a successful vet, or dog owner, you can't begin to recognise abnormal behaviour until you understand what's normal.

I ran up against authority again in my last year at St Leo's College (a residential college at the university) when I got into trouble for being outspoken and not toeing the line. I was president of the students' club, and I objected to the bans on alcohol and women in the college, so I told the Principal what I thought — I've never learned to curb my tongue. We had a number of run-ins, and the Principal told me if I didn't like the rules, I could leave. I have never resigned in my life, and I didn't back down then. An uneasy truce existed between the two of us for the rest of that year. The following year, after I had left, the college rules were changed, and I felt I had won a moral victory.

In my final year a breeder brought in a five-month-old Bull Terrier with a broken leg for treatment and I was given the case. When I told the breeder the dog needed an operation he said he couldn't afford to have it done. I asked if he would give me the dog rather than put it down, and he agreed, so at the end of the year I airfreighted Tigger the Bull Terrier down to Melbourne.

He was a typical Bull Terrier, game as Ned Kelly. He loved humans and was an absolute buffoon, but he detested all other animals, especially Labradors. He would pick a Labrador out of a pack of dogs and, being a battler, would tear off to fight it. His party piece was to roar around, hyping himself up, then he'd get hysterical chasing his tail. After all that he'd collapse, having put on what he thought was a wonderful circus show.

Tigger was the first dog I owned who confirmed for me a lifelong love of terriers. He loved acting and entertaining humans, but there was also a sinister side to him. When people he didn't like came to the house he would stand at the end of the drive and stare them out. People were terrified of him.

He would go everywhere with me in my Ford Anglia. Of all the dogs I've owned, he was the one who responded most to my emotions. If I was upset he'd push his head into me and look through those funny eyes, saying, 'Look, I know you're upset, but I'm here, too.'

Terriers are very loyal and they bond very closely to you. It's terrific to get home and have them say, 'About bloody time. We've got a few things to do.' I like their liveliness and go-get-it approach to life, which in some ways mirrors my own. They also have an aggressive streak if their peace is disturbed.

Lots of people declare themselves scared of me. Being President of the RSPCA, I believe I have to represent animals single-mindedly, without having to ingratiate myself with people, and I don't make myself easy to know. A lot of the time I stand there like Tigger, staring down my nose at the end of the driveway and saying, 'That's my position. I won't budge.'

In appearance, I'd say I resemble an Airedale — hairy, tweedy, and unkempt — but in attitude I'm like a Staffordshire Bull Terrier. They're more of a buffoon than an English Bull Terrier, but they never back off in a fight. They're not pretty to look at, but neither am I.

At Xavier College I had a friend whose father was a vet in the Victorian country town of Drouin in Gippsland. In the holidays I used to go down there to help him and carry his bag. An understanding developed that when I graduated I would go to work for him, so in 1964 I left Tigger and Rufus with my parents in Melbourne and went to live in the vet's house in Drouin. He had his own dogs, including one cross breed called Whelan, who was a wrecker, so there was no room for my dogs.

The bread and butter of the practice was dairy cows, and we only looked at dogs at night. Today there wouldn't be a rural practice in Australia which didn't depend on companion animals for its income. There had only been a veterinary practice in Drouin for 12 years and we had to let people know the services we could perform for animals. For instance, there was widespread ignorance that infectious diseases like distemper could be prevented by a simple vaccination. We saw dog after dog that hadn't been vaccinated.

I spent a lot of time treating the working dogs that rounded up the cows for milking twice a day. They weren't particularly well-treated, and the owners sometimes neglected their diet or other aspects of animal husbandry such as flea control. It was frequently frustrating to see how little impact I had: often my instructions about care were ignored. I was young, and seen as no better than an academic nitwit. It was often said to me that I'd done all the book learning, but not enough practical work.

The farmers all had Ferguson tractors with a scissor mower attachment. In November they would start cutting the grass for hay and, inevitably, a working dog would run up to the tractor and the mower would cut a paw off. I'd be confronted with a bleeding dog without a paw. The only thing I could do was amputate the leg properly so that the dog could continue on three legs. At least it taught me that animals do reasonably well with a leg removed.

After amputation the dog would be left with a wound that needed to be kept clean, particularly from cow dung, so the last thing I expected was for the farmer to send it straight back to the paddock to resume work. The farmers would say, 'Don't you realise it's a working dog?' and I would reply, 'Don't you realise it's had major surgery, and needs to be given a chance to recover?'

The owners used to get cross with me because I always came down on the side of the dogs. They thought, bloody Wirth has told me to lock up the dog for 10 days but he doesn't realise it's the only dog I have to bring in the cows. They weren't deliberately cruel; it was due to thoughtlessness. So few humans sit down and think of a different way of doing something.

It was a lesson in animal behaviour. If you're roaring round a paddock with a mower, of course a working dog like a Border Collie or a Kelpie will roar around too, trying to bite the wheels. Guess what happens if there's a mower? How many times do I still have to repair animals' feet and tails? It's an expensive way of teaching people to lock up the dog if you're mowing. Dog owners, like lots of people, don't like hearing the truth. I get into trouble for telling owners their dogs are overweight. The dog doesn't have a credit card at the supermarket, so who's responsible for giving it the food?

I didn't make myself popular at the nearby Ellinbank Dairy Research Unit, either. It was run by the Department of Agriculture, and was doing research on docking cows' tails. They wanted me to cut the calves' tails off and I refused, for the same reasons that I still get angry about docking the tails of dogs or cows. Why did God give them tails? It's another case of people trying to make animals suit human needs, rather than our adjusting to their needs.

No one in Drouin had ever seen surgical procedures like desexing, which I introduced. The vet had never even performed a caesarean on a cow. I let him know that I felt my veterinary standards were going backwards, and protested that I seemed to be working all hours of the day and night. As I told him all this when I was only 12 months out of veterinary school and he had been practising for 40 years, he did not take it too well. I left after 18 months and took a locum's position at the Balwyn veterinary practice, which had started in 1906. Because of ill health both vets, Phillip Kelynack and Nils Sjogren, retired within six months of my joining, and I took over the practice in 1965, at the age of 26.

Rufus the Irish Setter was 13 by that time and, as a vet, I recognised he had to be put down because of old age. I had to make the decision to put him down, but I wouldn't do it myself. I brought him into the practice a couple of weeks after I'd started the locum, and asked the other vets to do it, but I wouldn't let them do anything while I was on the premises. Rufus was the longest living dog I'd had, and it was very upsetting.

Whenever I lose a dog, I am left with a huge void. While I've been upset about the death of an animal, I don't think I've mourned one very long. It's right to mourn, but not to be maudlin. The dog you've lost is fixed in the memory and however cut up you are about the loss, there's always another dog out there waiting for you. People say they could never replace the dog they've just lost, and they couldn't go through the same grief again, but they're the ones who miss out if they don't get another dog. They would soon become attached to a new animal.

I bought another Irish Setter, Dhougal, to replace Rufus, and within a year he and Tigger were joined by a Gordon Setter pup called Fergus McPherson. A client had a Gordon Setter bitch and I went to see the dog after she'd had a litter of 13 pups. Gordon Setters were very scarce in those days. I was attracted to them straight away and decided to get one. Ever since then I've always had at least three dogs.

The vets at the Balwyn practice had done occasional work for the RSPCA, and I soon started doing public work for the organisation. In 1969 Noel Needham, the vet who was on the RSPCA council, resigned and I was nominated to replace him. I gave a lot of talks and, in 1972, the year after Tigger died, I went to the police academy at Glen Waverley to lecture on the Prevention of Cruelty Act and the handling of dogs and horses. I met a police sergeant there who taught law to the students and who had bought an Airedale. Soon after, he left the police force and went into a newsagency. One day he suddenly turned up in the surgery with the Airedale, saying he wanted to put it down because he couldn't stand it any more. He wanted to buy a Rottweiler. I asked if I might have the dog and he said, 'I don't care who has it, so long as I don't.'

There's something about Airedales. They're extremely loving and bond very closely, and they're just that little bit different from other terriers. Kit came with me in the front seat to every case I attended. Whenever I gave a human a lift, the person had to go in the back seat while Kit sat regally in the passenger seat.

The Balwyn practice dealt primarily with companion animals. I found a much better appreciation of veterinary science there than in Drouin, but there was still much ignorance about dog behaviour and what we could do to help. People still clung to the old wives' tales: that feeding milk to dogs caused worms; that raw meat caused distemper; and that the cure for dermatitis was to smear the skin with a mixture of lard and sulphur. In fact, sulphur was supposed to be good for most things wrong with dogs.

I was exposed to a large number of cases, and a large number of different owners. Apart from witnessing the strong bond between animal and owner, I also began to draw some conclusions about dog ownership. There was plenty of evidence to support the saying that dogs become like their owners, and it was equally obvious that people selected dogs as an extension of their personality, often to compensate in those areas where they considered themselves wanting. I found, for example, that law-enforcement officers liked large, powerful dogs.

I became increasingly fond of terriers and, after I had lost the two setters, Dhougal and Fergus, I bought Joshua, my first Cairn Terrier. I had grown to like the breed through my work at the practice, and I was later given a second Cairn, Jonah. When Kit died of cancer in 1987 I replaced her with a second Airedale, Kate. Sheelagh, the Irish Terrier, arrived in 1991.

INTRODUCTION

Sheelagh was the first dog I'd ever had select me. I'd always wanted an Irish Terrier, and as soon as the breeder rang to tell me about the litter I went out to the farm to look at the five pups. Sheelagh kept coming back to sit on my foot. She'd decided to come home to Balwyn, and that made my mind up.

With four dogs, I now needed a car big enough to drive them around. Rufus was the only dog I'd ever owned who was car sick. Most dogs love the sense of movement in a car, and seeing things out of the window. The car becomes part of their extended territory and arouses their possessiveness. Some dogs are so obsessive about cars that they will jump in and wait for hours for it to go.

Dogs make cars dirty and I needed a clean conveyance for formal occasions, so my solution was to have two cars, one to take the dogs and one in which the dogs are forbidden. I decided to buy a utility with a cabin big enough for the dogs, and went off to a showroom to find something I liked. When I'd done that I told the salesman I'd buy the car provided the children approved.

I drove home, picked up the dogs and took them down to the garage. The salesman was horrified when he saw that the sale depended on the approval of four terriers. I spelled out the terms of the deal: 'Either they get into the ute and show me they're happy, or there's no sale.' Reluctantly the salesman let the dogs get in, and they immediately took up positions, ready to go. I told the salesman, 'It looks like you've sold me a ute!'

The dogs always know when it's Saturday morning and time to drive into Melbourne for my radio broadcast on 3LO (now 774 ABC Melbourne). I park next to the studios and leave the dogs in the car. One Saturday the ABC doorman came into the studio to tell me I'd left the radio on in the car. Of course I'd left the bloody radio on. Couldn't he see that the dogs were listening?

1

Your new dog

SELECTING YOUR PERFECT PARTNER

So many problems of dog ownership, and the dumping of unwanted dogs, stem from the fact that people buy through the heart, not the head. When they see the eight-week-old puppy in the pet shop, they don't consider how that dog will behave when it's a year old. All puppies are beautiful, but they grow up with the characteristics of their breed, and often people don't consider whether those characteristics will suit their personality and lifestyle.

The problem we face with companion animals is that humans need them for sanity, but because we've become heavily urbanised, we often don't understand them. People have begun to understand the care of dogs, and the message 'worm, groom, vaccinate' has got through, but we haven't had the same success with the message that people must train their dogs, and give careful thought to breed selection.

Before you buy

There are a million reasons people buy dogs, and most of them are the wrong ones. Few people consider whether the particular breed would complement their personality, and whether their lifestyle would allow them to spend time with the dog and walk it. Instead people say, 'I must have a Basset Hound, because I saw one on television, and it looked cute.' Or they see a magazine article on the latest fashionable dog breeds such as an Alaskan Malamute, Australian Shepherd, Bouvier Des Flandres, Shar Pei, Pyrenean Mountain Dog, or Australian Cattle Dog, and determine to buy a puppy to become the talk of the district without having any understanding of the chosen breed and its behavioural characteristics. Impulse buying is a major source of problems reflected in the number of currently fashionable breeds found in animal shelters and pounds.

People recognise that races have unique characteristics but, for some reason, don't apply the same thinking to dogs. They believe all dogs will behave in exactly the same way. Before you buy, study the types of dog that would best suit you. Go to a library and read the latest books on dogs, and study the synopsis on each breed, and the reason the dog was originally bred. It will tell you exactly what to expect of the animal when it's an adult dog.

For instance, if you buy a working dog, you must expect a dog with the potential to bite, because they nip cattle when they round them up. It will also have limitless energy and be willing to work all day long. People buy a cattle dog, put it on a quarter-acre block, walk it for an hour at the weekend and wonder why the dog is going bananas. Working dogs were bred to look after stock, and they're energetic, highly intelligent, brain-active dogs.

'Selectapet' programme
The Petcare Information and Advisory Service (PIAS) in each state runs a free 'Selectapet' computer programme,

which will match up your needs and lifestyle with an appropriate breed. People are given a questionnaire and asked to give answers on their present accommodation, how much exercise and grooming they are prepared to give the dog each day, the amount of time it would be required to spend on its own, the weekly budget for food, and whether it is required to guard the property. The replies are then matched with the characteristics of different breeds and the person is given a choice of four suitable breeds, together with breed cards illustrating and describing the dog.

The breed alternatives are presented with the following salutary advice:

> We realise that beauty is in the eye of the beholder, but do not dismiss a breed from consideration merely because you may not care initially for the look of the pet in the photo. You are choosing a companion with whom to share life's ups and downs, not a fashion accessory, and as such your decision should be based on mutual suitability, rather than aesthetic appeal or any preconceived notions regarding a particular breed.

The cost of bad choices

If you make the wrong selection you will never be happy with the dog, and it's no good abandoning the animal six months later and leaving it to the local pound or RSPCA to solve your wrong choice. Some people give away unwanted dogs, and some just dump them. They may push the dog out of the car on a deserted country road after dark, or simply leave the back gate open on purpose and then make no effort to go and find the dog. However it's done, dumping is an offence under the Prevention of Cruelty to Animals Act, which says that a person is guilty of cruelty if he or she 'abandons an animal of a species usually kept in a state of confinement or for a domestic purpose'. The penalty is a $14,000 fine or 12 months' imprisonment.

It's a crime against a dog to buy it as a puppy and then abandon it a few months later because it doesn't suit you any more. Dogs are almost entirely dependent on humans and, when you dump them, there's no certainty that their dependency will be met. That's where the cruelty is involved.

The RSPCA alone has to put down about 1000 animals a week in Australia, and most of those deaths are caused by people selecting the wrong dog or failing to train their pets. If you make the wrong choice and you haven't trained the dog, you may grow to dislike it intensely. The trigger for getting rid of it may be that it suddenly bites someone, so the owner has it destroyed or dumps it. Half of all the dogs brought in to the RSPCA will be destroyed because homes cannot be found for them.

Know the breed characteristics

Often when a dog bites it is displaying the inherent breed characteristics. For example, Corgis will bite because they are cattle dogs, and they nip cows. Bull Terriers were bred to fight other dogs, and it doesn't take much for them to switch from gregarious buffoons to fighting mode. If a Bull Terrier kills a child it's a tragedy, but, for me, part of the tragedy is that the dog's owners failed to see the aggression inherent in the breed and take precautions to prevent it. If I owned a Rottweiler or a Pit Bull Terrier, I could never say it's so well-bred that it will never attack another dog, or a human. How the dog fits into the wider society is the true test of its behaviour and how well socialised it is, not how it reacts to its owner.

People often complain about the yapping of terriers, but that is a characteristic of the breed. Terriers are earth dogs bred to flush out foxes and other animals from their dens. They are sharp and alert and you must expect them to dig in the garden and to bark or yap, which is their alerting mechanism.

Dogs are often selected on the basis of the owners' views of themselves. The tizzy blonde with dripping jewellery will always have a Poodle. The small, muscular bloke wearing a blue singlet and covered with tattoos always has a Bull Terrier at the end of his arm. The moustachioed police-inspector types are heavily into Dobermanns and Rottweilers. German Shepherds are usually owned by people who want to be dominant. The longer you work in veterinary practice, the more you see that these truisms are supported by reality.

Cross breed or pure breed?

Roughly half the dogs in Australia are cross breeds, and they can be just as good companions as pure breeds. There is a genetic tendency for a cross breed to have the good points of both breeds, and you get what is called 'hybrid vigour', a result of mixing the narrower gene pool of each of the breeds. One result is greater longevity, and another is that you often end up with a healthier animal, because you avoid many of the genetically inherited complaints which are specific to a particular breed. For instance, poodles have breed-specific problems with their eyes, mouths, hearts and knees. If you cross a poodle with another breed, the puppy that results will probably not have these faults to such a degree. The main difference with a pure breed is that you acquire predictable looks, temperament and behaviour; the same predictability does not occur with cross breeds.

Designer dogs — dog hybrids

In the early 1980s Guide Dogs Victoria commenced a breeding program crossing a Labrador with a Standard Poodle hoping to produce a healthy guide dog of even temperament and low coat shedding. This hybrid cross became known as a Labradoodle and soon became a popular choice as a pet dog. Other hybrid crosses followed such as the Groodle (Golden Retriever – Standard Poodle) and smaller types Spoodle (Miniature Poodle – Spaniel), Cavoodle (Cavalier King Charles Spaniel – Miniature Poodle) and the very popular Maltese – Miniature Poodle. A survey in 2007 concluded that hybrid cross dogs were 10 per cent of the pet dog population in Australia.

Most of these hybrids are medium-sized, bright, intelligent, healthy dogs with a consistently good temperament. They are a welcome addition to the world of dogs available as pets.

Buying a puppy

When we buy a puppy we should give the decision just as much consideration as if we were buying a house or a car, but few people going to buy a puppy take along someone who knows about dogs. Make sure you look at the surroundings and how the puppy is presented; check that the dog is a minimum of eight weeks old and that it has the right certification.

Many dogs have congenital inherited defects, so when you go to buy the dog you should use your eyes, seek advice and don't always trust what you're told. German Shepherds, for instance, are well-known for having skeletal problems, and Dobermanns have spinal problems. Say you will buy the dog subject to a veterinary check. Victorian vets offer the 'Vetcheck' service, in which they will inspect a pup and give a written assessment for the normal consultation fee. Breeders are proud, competitive people, and they may not like it, but this is the age of consumerism. I've spent 30 years dealing with animals from shonky breeders.

Puppies show their temperament very quickly, and it's there to be seen. They show it in the way they come up to you as a stranger. If they're fearful, suspicious or don't like to be handled — all signs of a poor temperament — don't have anything to do with them. If you do, you're buying trouble. It's often the people who buy the dogs with poor temperaments who give up on them.

RSPCA Smart Puppy-Buyer's Guide

HEALTHY PUPPIES COME FROM BREEDERS WHO:
1. Plan ahead and aim to find good homes for every puppy they breed
2. Provide a high standard of care and living conditions for all their dogs
3. Are genuinely concerned about the welfare of their dogs
4. Are open to questions and provide a complete history of the puppy
5. Make sure that you will suit the puppy and the puppy will suit you
6. Breed to produce happy, healthy pets, free from known genetic disorders
7. Provide ongoing support and information to new owners
8. Provide a guarantee
9. Provide references on request
10. Meet all their legal requirements

Finding a good breeder means asking questions

1. DID THE BREEDER PLAN AHEAD FOR THIS LITTER?
A responsible dog breeder plans each pregnancy and knows that there is enough demand for their puppies to ensure they will all go to good homes.

Ask the breeder if this pregnancy was planned, how many litters the mother has already had (six should be the maximum over her whole life), and what they will do with any unsold puppies (a good breeder will hang on to them until the right home can be found).

2. ARE YOU IMPRESSED WITH THE STANDARD OF CARE AND LIVING CONDITIONS OF THE DOGS?

It's really important that you visit the puppy in the place where it was born and meet its mum (and dad too, if he's around).

- Check whether the place is clean and there is enough space for the puppies and adult dogs to move around and exercise and there are things for the pups to chew on and play with.
- Ask what the puppies are fed and how often. A good breeder will provide information on how to feed your puppy before you take it home.
- Ask about health checks, worming and vaccinations, and what documents will come home with your puppy. A good breeder will make sure all puppies have a full veterinary health check and are microchipped, vaccinated and treated for worms and fleas before they are sold, and will provide you with records of these treatments.
- Watch how the puppies and the adult dogs in the home behave — are they friendly with people and other

dogs? A good breeder will make sure the puppies and breeding dogs are friendly and well-socialised.

If the breeder is reluctant for you to visit, or wants you to meet the puppy in another place, find another breeder. Puppy farms will often use a house as a 'shop front' so you don't get to see the poor conditions they breed dogs in. Don't buy a puppy from a pet shop or through an internet or newspaper advertisement without being able to visit its home, as you can't check out the conditions in which the puppy was bred or know where it came from.

> **PUPPY FARMS**
>
> A puppy mill or puppy farm is a mass-production facility that breeds puppies for profit. The puppies and their mothers are often kept in very poor conditions. Breeding animals may be continually mated and kept with their puppies in cages and never allowed out to exercise, play, have companionship or even go to the toilet. Puppies born in puppy farms often have long-term health and behavioural problems as a result of poor housing conditions, poor maternal nutrition and a lack of adequate socialisation during the crucial first few weeks of life.

3. IS THE BREEDER GENUINELY CONCERNED ABOUT THE WELFARE OF THEIR DOGS?

Good breeders want the best for all their animals, from new puppies to retired breeding dogs. They take steps to ensure this by providing detailed advice to new owners about how to care for their puppy, and don't have old breeding dogs put down because they're no longer productive.

- Ask the breeder what happens to their retired breeding animals — are they kept or rehomed?
- If the breed you've chosen was traditionally docked, what is the breeder's view on tail docking? (Routine tail docking of puppies is no longer legal in Australia.)
- If you are not intending to breed from your puppy, the breeder should provide advice on desexing (unless your puppy has been desexed already).

You should be provided with information on diet, socialisation, registration and identification requirements, and any medications or vaccinations given or required in the future.

4. IS THE BREEDER OPEN TO QUESTIONS AND DO THEY PROVIDE A COMPLETE HISTORY OF THE PUPPY?

Good breeders want to make sure you are well-informed about your new puppy and will provide information on the background, size, breed and temperament of his parents.

They are willing to answer questions and allow inspection of records and paperwork such as registration documents and veterinary records. A breeder who refuses to answer reasonable questions probably has something to hide.

5. DOES THE BREEDER MAKE SURE YOU WILL SUIT THE PUPPY AND THE PUPPY WILL SUIT YOU?

A new puppy is a long-term commitment, so both you and the breeder need to be certain you are making the right decision. A good breeder will ask you questions to make sure this is the right puppy for you and that you're able to care for it properly.

For example, they might ask:

- if you have children or other animals in the household,
- where your puppy will be sleeping, and
- how often it will be left on its own.

They should also tell you what to expect from the breed, such as how suitable it is for families and how much space and exercise is needed. If you're at all uncomfortable with what you are told, you might want to consider another breed.

6. IS YOUR PUPPY BRED TO BE A PET AND FREE FROM KNOWN INHERITED DISORDERS?

Different breeds are predisposed to different inherited disorders or diseases. Some of these aren't apparent until later in a dog's life but can have devastating consequences. Some breeds also have exaggerated features that can cause problems, like a squashed-in face, which makes it hard to breathe, or very short legs, which can lead to spinal problems.

A good breeder will be aware of, and screen for, any known disorders or anatomical problems specific to the breed and will exclude dogs with problems from breeding. They will be able to show you copies of veterinary reports and screening tests to confirm this. They should also breed to minimise any exaggerated physical traits specific to the breed that are known to have an adverse impact on the health and welfare of the dog.

- Find out what inherited diseases occur in your chosen breed (an internet search for inherited diseases and the breed name will help you) and ask the breeder what steps they have taken to prevent them.
- One proven way to minimise the risk of inherited problems is to avoid breeding closely related animals. If you are buying a purebred dog, you should check your puppy's pedigree to make sure there are no close relative matings, such as brother–sister or grandfather–granddaughter matings.
- Ask the breeder what they think are the most important characteristics in their puppies. A good breeder will put health, welfare and temperament above appearance. Some breeders put success in the show ring above all else, but breed prizes such as 'best in show' don't mean that a dog's puppies will be good family pets as

show dogs are judged on their appearance, not their behaviour.

7. DOES THE BREEDER OFFER TO PROVIDE ONGOING SUPPORT AND INFORMATION AFTER PURCHASE?

A good breeder will provide full contact details and encourage you to get in touch if you need more information on the care of your new puppy.

8. DOES THE BREEDER PROVIDE A GUARANTEE?

What if you take the puppy home and it has a health problem, or doesn't get on with your children or pet cat and you can't cope? A good breeder will offer to take back unwanted animals within a specified time period after sale. They should also offer to accept animals returned as a result of problems arising from an inherited disorder at any time after sale.

9. DOES THE BREEDER PROVIDE REFERENCES TO BACK UP WHAT THEY HAVE TOLD YOU?

You might have asked a lot of questions so far, but you'd like to be absolutely sure that the breeder is genuine. A good breeder will readily provide references on request, including testimonials from previous or existing owners, letters from the vet, and documents indicating membership of a breed association, canine council or companion animal club.

10. IS THE BREEDER MEETING ALL LEGAL REQUIREMENTS?

Requirements for dog breeders vary from state to state, but it's a good idea to call your local council and ask whether breeders have to be registered with them and if there is a code of practice or guidelines that they should be following. If the answer's yes, you can ask the breeder for their registration details and what guidelines they follow.

> ### REGISTERED BREEDERS
> Pedigree or purebred dog breeders are often referred to as 'registered breeders' when they are members of a breed club or association that operates a stud book or register. The term may also be used to refer to someone who is registered with their local council as a breeder (also called a 'recognised' breeder).
>
> While breed associations do have rules and guidelines for their members, being 'registered' does not necessarily mean a breeder is responsible or meets good animal welfare standards. To make sure your breeder is a good breeder, you need to ask the right questions before you buy.

If your breeder meets the RSPCA's Smart Puppy-Buyer's Guide, congratulations!

Thanks to their excellent care and breeding practices, your puppy has had a great start in life — the rest is up to you. Before you take your puppy home, check out the RSPCA's information on puppy training and make sure you talk to your local vet about desexing!

BREEDS

Dog breeds fall into seven main groupings: toys, terriers, gun-dogs, hounds, working dogs, utility breeds and non-sporting dogs. When you have decided which breed you want, your vet will be able to suggest how you can get in touch with breeders. Failing that you can contact your state's canine association, which will have a list of clubs for the different breeds.

Toy dogs

The best-known toy dogs are the Australian Silky Terrier, the Bichon Frise, the Cavalier King Charles Spaniel, the Chihuahua, the Maltese, the Pekingese, the Pomeranian, the Pug and the Yorkshire Terrier. Most of these dogs were bred specifically to be pets and lap dogs. In many cases the dogs had attention lavished on them by the royal families of Europe and China, and even featured in court paintings.

The common characteristic of all these toy dogs is that they are small, and can easily be nursed and carried, and as a result of this they are often highly dependent, developing an intense, personal, one-to-one relationship with their owners. They are usually 'boss dogs', and their owners let them get away with murder. Very subtly, they can become the dominant partner. They do not need much exercise.

BICHON FRISE

The Bichon Frise figured in the paintings of the 17th-century Spanish artist Murillo. This small, fluffy, white dog (the word *frise* means curly-coated) was brought to France from Tenerife, in the Spanish Canary Islands, and it was kept by French kings and aristocrats. It lost status at the end of the 19th century, when its role changed to circus performer and organ grinder's dog, but it has increased rapidly in popularity in recent years. Its happy nature makes it an ideal family pet.

CAVALIER KING CHARLES SPANIEL

English chroniclers of the time said that King Charles II preferred the company of his spaniels to that of human beings. The diarist Samuel Pepys wrote that the monarch 'often suffered the bitches to puppy and give suck, which rendered it very offensive and indeed made the whole court nasty and stinking'. The king's dogs formed part of the early history of the popular Cavalier King Charles Spaniel, which was developed in the 1920s by an American breeder. The breed is affectionate, domesticated and well-suited to living indoors.

CHIHUAHUA

The Mexican Chihuahua is said to be descended from the sacred dog of the Aztecs. Christopher Columbus reported that he found small, domesticated dogs on his explorations of Mexico, but the Chihuahua did not reach the US until the 1890s, almost 400 years later. It soon became the top toy dog in the US, and has since become one of the most popular dogs in the world. Its tiny body hides a large heart, and its playful, alert character has endeared it as a companion to the elderly and people living in apartments. There is a smooth-coated Chihuahua, and a long-coated variety, which probably resulted from crosses with the Papillon or Pomeranian.

MALTESE

The Maltese, which originated in the Mediterranean island of Malta, was also depicted in Italian paintings. It is thought to be the oldest of the European toy breeds, and Aristotle made mention of the fact that the dog came from Malta. It was imported into Britain at the time of Henry VIII and well established as a pet dog by the 19th century. These small dogs were prized for their good nature, intelligence and attentiveness to their owners, and it was a common sight to see women holding them in their laps when they travelled in carriages. Their long, white silky coat makes them cute and cuddly, like the Bichon.

PEKINGESE

The Pekingese is the original pampered pooch. Known as the royal dog of China, the animals have been recorded in China since the Tang dynasty of the eighth century, but they became the darlings of the Chinese imperial court in the 19th century, when a force of 4000 eunuchs were housed in Peking to breed and raise the dogs, and stealing a Pekingese was an offence punishable by death. Two 'pekes' used to announce the appearance of the Emperor with short, sharp barks.

When Peking was sacked by the British in 1860, five dogs were transported back to England and one of them was given to Queen Victoria. The breed, with its flat face, shortened muzzle, prominent eyes and fluffy coat, quickly grew in popularity as it made a confident, charming companion with a tendency to stubbornness. The dog's lion-like appearance sometimes led to it being known in China as the 'lion dog', but it was also credited with possessing the heart of a lion, and it would never turn tail if attacked. The eunuchs of Peking would sometimes entertain themselves by staging fights between the dogs.

POMERANIAN

The Pomeranian is the smallest of the spitz group of dogs, which were descended from the sledge-hauling dogs of the Arctic countries. The dogs took their name from the region of Pomerania, in Germany, where they were bred. They were gradually reduced in size, and also developed from white coats to reds, oranges, and browns. Queen Victoria helped introduce the dogs to England when she took some home from a visit to Germany in 1888, and their vivacious and affectionate nature has made them popular family pets and excellent companions for children or elderly people.

PUG

The Pug also originated in China. It was derived from the Mastiff, with a large head, wrinkled face and heavyweight body. The origin of the name has been the subject of keen debate, with some historians saying it comes from the Latin word *pugnus*, meaning a fist, as the dog's head resembles a clenched human fist. The breed is thought to have been introduced to Holland by Dutch traders who visited China in the 16th century, and it later became popular in England, where Queen Victoria favoured the dogs. Pugs were friendly and quick to attach themselves to households. They even became a permanent fixture in some families when stuffing the family pet became fashionable.

YORKSHIRE TERRIER

The Yorkshire Terrier first appeared in England around 1850, but it was not given this name until 1870. The Yorkshireman spent his days in the pits and mills and his weekends hunting vermin with his terrier, and a variety of the dogs were bred in the English county. The 'Yorkie' is probably a cross of the old English black-and-tan terriers, the Skye Terrier and the Maltese. Originally a larger, hardier dog, the Yorkie has since become smaller, with a silkier coat, but the decrease in size has not affected its spirit or self-confidence. It is quick to sound the alarm and makes an affectionate companion.

Terriers

The terrier group includes the Airedale, Australian, Bull, Cairn, Fox, Irish, Jack Russell, Scottish, Staffordshire Bull and West Highland White. They are game, loyal dogs that were bred to flush foxes, rats, rabbits or badgers out of burrows. They are highly alert, keyed-up, feisty, and fearless. They were bred to spend hours in the field hunting, so they need above-average exercise. They snap and yap because they're alert, and regard everything as foreign. They're dominant and need to be dominated back. Sheelagh, my Irish Terrier, would like to be the boss dog, but I've told her that's not on. They can become great attention-seekers.

AIREDALE
The Airedale, which is described as the king of the terriers, was also bred in Yorkshire, in the valley of the river Aire, around the 1850s. The dog was bred for ratting and hunting foxes, weasels and badgers, and resulted from a cross of the Otterhound and the hard-coated black-and-tan terrier. It was used by the British Army to carry messages in the First World War, when it acquired a reputation for intelligence, character and devotion to duty.

BORDER TERRIER
The Border Terrier essentially remains a working terrier in its country of origin, the border districts of Scotland. Despite this apparent self-assurance the Border remains a sensitive dog, companionable by nature and they take a very keen interest in everything that is going on.

They are smart little dogs that provide me with all of the joys of dog ownership that I am used to with terriers.

BULL TERRIER
The Bull Terrier resulted from crossing the old English white terrier, the Bulldog and the Staffordshire Bull Terrier, and in its early days it was used as a ratter and fighter. In the words of the British breeder and show judge Harry Glover, the Bull Terrier 'was considered to be the associate of low fellows'. The breed was lifted above its humble

origins by a Birmingham dog dealer, James Hinks, who produced a more distinguished all-white dog. Although the dog makes an affectionate companion, it is a fearless defender of property, and has been described as the gladiator of the canine race. Although it can be aggressive with other dogs or animals, it acts like a buffoon with humans. The Staffordshire Bull Terrier resulted from the crossing of the Bulldog and the old English smooth terrier.

CAIRN TERRIER

The Cairn Terrier is a native of the western highlands of Scotland, and takes its name from the pile of rocks erected to identify a boundary or to mark a grave. These cairns became favourite hiding places for foxes and other vermin, and the terriers would dig their way in among the stones to drive out the foxes. The dogs are hard-coated, independent, curious, energetic and sturdy enough to face up to strong adversaries.

FOX TERRIER

The Fox Terrier also has a sturdy character, and is just as good standing up to the enthusiastic handling of it by young children as it is pursuing foxes down their holes. The dog has an irrepressible spirit, and its staying power, eyesight and keen nose have made it a highly prized sporting dog. In the earliest days of fox hunting, the terriers were often carried by the riders in boxes or sacks, and only released after the larger foxhounds had driven the quarry to gound. It was then up to the Fox Terrier to flush the foxes out of their lairs.

The dog can either be smooth- or wire-coated. The smooth-coated dog is thought to have been bred from the smooth-coated black-and-tan terrier, with subsequent infusions of Beagle, Bulldog and Greyhound; the Greyhound providing the breed's characteristic long nose.

IRISH AND SCOTTISH TERRIERS

Ireland and Scotland both produced their own terriers. The Irish Terrier has become known for its distinctive red coat and the devilish streak to its nature. Hence its nickname 'the red devil'. The dogs were originally bred for sporting purposes, but they were frequently matched against each other in fights. They are staunchly loyal, protective of property, adapt easily to surroundings, and love to press themselves on their owners for attention. The black Scottish Terrier with its short legs and heavy build is less glamorous than its Irish cousin, but is loyal, determined and dour.

Colonel E D Malcolm of Poltalloch, in Scotland, first drew attention to the West Highland White Terriers in the 19th century, after he had been breeding them for 60 years to cope with the difficult terrain of the region. Their self-assured, playful nature has made them increasingly popular ever since, and they have also had considerable success as show dogs.

JACK RUSSELL TERRIER

The Jack Russell is named after the Reverend Jack Russell, a passionate English fox hunter of the mid-1800s. The Reverend Russell liked a longer-legged terrier that could follow the hounds on foot, and he is reported to have developed his own strain, based on a cross bred terrier bitch he bought from a milkman. The dog he produced was game and spirited and loved to hunt and rat.

Gun dogs

Gun dogs originated in Europe from around the 17th century, when more sophisticated guns became available to shoot game. They were divided into different groups, according to the purpose for which they were bred. Setters and pointers would locate the game; spaniels whose job it was to 'spring' the game, getting the birds to fly into the air, or driving the rabbits out of their holes and making them run; retrievers would bring back the wounded or dead game to the shooter. The various gun dogs include the Cocker and Springer Spaniels, English, Irish and Gordon Setters, English Pointer, German Short-haired Pointer, Golden Retriever, Labrador and Weimaraner.

RETRIEVERS

Much of the work in developing the retriever breeds was done in England in the 19th century, although Germany had the Weimaraner, which was the sporting dog of the court of Weimar. Early last century the water dogs from the east coast of Canada were keenly sought by English shooters, who were looking for dogs to retrieve water fowl. One that impressed buyers was the long-coated Newfoundland, a relative of the Swiss St Bernard. Through careful breeding, a smooth-coated, water-loving dog called the Labrador Retriever was established, and named after the area of Canada close to Newfoundland.

The Newfoundland was also crossed with setters and spaniels to produce the long-coated Golden Retriever. They were large, strong, intelligent dogs with a love of water, the will to work, a capacity to bond closely with their owner, and a gentle, tolerant nature, which has since made them enormously popular as pets.

SETTERS AND POINTERS

The setters would 'set' the game by suddenly freezing, like a statue, in the presence of game. Setting dogs were recorded in England in the 16th century, but much of the development of the English Setter took place in the 19th century. The Fourth Duke of Gordon, who lived in Scotland from 1743 to 1827, is usually given credit for breeding the black-and-tan Gordon Setters. The Irish, or Red Setter, is a deep chestnut colour, and has the graceful, flowing appearance of its English and Scottish relatives.

Like the spaniel group of dogs, the pointer is thought to have originated in Spain, where it became famous during the early 17th century for its ability to point to the bird with its nose, body and tail in a straight line. The earliest pointers were slow and heavy, but they were later crossed with different French hounds to produce the German Short-haired Pointer. An English Pointer was also bred.

SPANIELS

In 1801 spaniels were divided into 'starters' and 'cockers'. The larger starter was used to spring the game while the smaller cocker was supposed to hunt the woodcock. The English Springer spaniels were included in the former group, and they proved themselves good hunters and retrievers, and excellent in water. What they may lack in intelligence, they make up for with their even temperament. They love to attach themselves to a family, and to lie by the fire. The Cocker Spaniel is an equally popular pet and, like the springer, few are now trained to work with guns.

A gentle nature is a characteristic of gun dogs. They needed to be soft-mouthed so that they could retrieve dead or injured game without bruising it. Some people equate their softness with brainlessness, or even a wimpish nature, but this is far from the truth. They need plenty of exercise because they were bred to hunt game by sweeping backwards and forwards across the paddocks.

Hounds

The hounds include the Afghan, the Basenji, the Basset, the Beagle, the Bloodhound, the Dachshund, the Deerhound, the Foxhound, the Greyhound, the Harrier, the Rhodesian Ridgeback and the Whippet. All were bred to chase game, and to pull it down. They would chase until the game was holed up, or until they caught and killed it. They have good eyesight, are quick to detect movement and, in a domestic situation, they can want to chase other animals.

AFGHAN

The Afghan is one of the oldest members of the Greyhound family, and, like the Basenji, the African hunting dog, it dates back thousands of years. Legend has it that the

Afghan was the dog Noah took into the ark. Once known as the Eastern Greyhound, the breed is thought to have originated in the Middle East, but subsequently made its way to the mountains of Afghanistan, where it was used to hunt wolves, foxes, gazelles, deer and goats, and to guard and herd sheep. Its long hair protected it against the extreme cold of the mountains.

The breed was imported into the US and Britain around the end of the 1800s, and its beauty and aristocratic bearing made it a popular show dog. It is not always amenable to discipline, and can sometimes appear aloof, but it can be a great clown at play time. Its basic instinct is to chase, and it needs plenty of exercise.

BASENJI

The short-haired Basenji, with its distinctive ring tail and wrinkling between the ears, is a small African dog that was used as a hunter, tracker and watchdog. It trots like a horse, and yodels instead of barking. Its name comes from the Bantu word meaning 'native of the bush' and the breed was discovered in central Africa by Western explorers in the late 1800s. Its strong pack instinct often leads to scrapping and bickering over the pecking order. The breed is semi-domesticated and although it is often cheeky and mischievous, its unpredictability of mood has prevented it becoming popular as a pet.

BASSET AND BEAGLE

The Basset and the Beagle both date back to the 16th century. The Basset, which is highly dominant, is thought to have originated in France. Queen Elizabeth I used to hunt with Beagles, and Shakespeare wrote about them. Like the larger Harrier, which was first used in packs in 18th-century England, the Beagle's primary role was to hunt hare. Both the Beagle and Foxhound are colony dogs, preferring to live in a group of other dogs. Beagles have not completed the transition to using humans as surrogate dogs, and while they will stay with humans, they prefer dogs and will often wander from home to look for other canine company.

BLOODHOUND
The Bloodhound is descended from an old breed introduced into England from Normandy by William the Conqueror in the 11th century. It was subsequently used to hunt red deer, and as a medieval patrol dog, employed to enforce the curfew. More recently it was used by police as a tracking dog because of its legendary powers of smell.

DACHSHUND
The Dachshund has many terrier characteristics even though it is classified as a hound. It has been given the disparaging nickname of 'sausage dog', because of its long body and short legs. Its name means 'badger dog' in German, and it was originally used to trail badgers, foxes, hares and rabbits into their burrows. The dogs hunt by scent, and still love a rabbit chase, but they have become popular as pets, being intelligent, self-willed, devoted to their owners and diffident with strangers. The breed

suffers from a spinal weakness which can lead to hind-leg paralysis. This fact has reduced its popularity in recent years. There are standard and miniature Dachshunds, with three different coat types: smooth, wire-haired or longhaired.

GREYHOUND AND WHIPPET
The Greyhound had been used for the sport of coursing or chasing rabbits in Greek and Roman times. The Whippet is a smaller version of the Greyhound, mixed with some blood from the Manchester and English white terriers. Both breeds are well-known for racing, and the Whippet has been highly successful as a domestic pet, being affectionate, intelligent and rarely aggressive.

RHODESIAN RIDGEBACK
The Rhodesian Ridgeback is also known as the Rhodesian lion dog, as it was originally created to track lions. It is believed to have resulted from crossing the Bloodhound with the Hottentot hunting dog, the latter breed giving the ridge of hair running down its back. By instinct these dogs are aggressive hunters and for this reason they are not ideal pets.

Working dogs
The working dogs include the Australian Cattle Dog, Collies, Corgis, the German Shepherd, the Kelpie, and the Old English Sheepdog. They were bred to assist humans to deal with stock, and to work over long hours and distances. They're built with a frame strong enough for

them to start working the paddocks at dawn and keep going straight through to dusk. They like to be occupied all the time, therefore directing the movement of stock is ideal work for them. It becomes rather like a game that they play continuously — they have to resolve the problem over and over again, to bring order out of chaos.

Working dogs need the most exercise of all dogs and, put in a suburban situation, they should be walked at least five kilometres a day. Instinctively they're always looking to move the sheep, and cattle, and if there is no stock in the back yard, they may want to play with a stick or tennis ball all day to satisfy their compulsion to work. Working people living in the city would be better suited to a more sedentary type of dog, like a Dachshund, Whippet, Poodle, Maltese or Shih Tzu.

Working dogs bond strongly with humans, but they must be dominated by the human, and the rules must be adhered to rigidly. They are very loyal, and that loyalty is usually proportional to the boss dog's dominance. They know their place, and they get frustrated if the rules aren't set. The dog does the work and its reward is that the owner provides food and housing.

COLLIES

Collies originate from the dogs used by the shepherds and farmers of Scotland to herd their sheep and cattle. The Bearded Collie has a long, shaggy coat which protects it against harsh weather, and which is similar to that of the Old English Sheepdog. It is a lively, even-tempered breed that loves exercise. It makes an affectionate, gentle, well-mannered pet and an intelligent worker. It has sometimes been described as temperamentally softer than some of the other working breeds.

The Border Collie originated in the border country between England and Scotland, where it was used as a sheepdog. It quickly became prized for its untiring willingness to work, its speed and agility and its alert and attentive manner. The breed is well-known for its piercing gaze, which has a hypnotic, controlling effect on sheep. This breed is also famous for its loyalty, and a story is told of a Border Collie that stood guard over his dead master in England for several days after the shepherd had died while working in the hills with his flock. The breed has become popular as a household pet, but the dogs can have a workaholic streak, derived from their instinctive desire to round up sheep, and they can be driven to herd anything or anyone.

The Rough Collie, with its distinctive, elongated nose, has become known as the 'Lassie dog', after the famous television series starring a Rough Collie. The dog originated in the lowlands of Scotland, and probably took its name from the local black sheep known as the colley. The long, aristocratic nose is thought to have come from a cross with a Russian Borzoi. The breed received its first increase in popularity in England in the late 19th century, after Queen Victoria had seen the dogs while staying at her Scottish estate at Balmoral, and took some back to Windsor Castle. The dogs are good-natured, affectionate, and as loyal to their owner and family as they can be suspicious of strangers.

All of the Collies can occasionally be short-tempered and 'nippy', traits which come from their herding instinct.

CORGIS
Welsh farmers bred Corgis to herd sheep and cows by nipping at their heels. They are believed to have some Nordic blood and look similar to the Swedish Vallhund, which has the same short legs and long body. The Cardigan Corgi is slightly larger and longer-bodied, while the Pembrokeshire Corgi is more foxy in appearance. The dogs are bold, full of self-importance and they make excellent guard dogs. Even though they love exercise and country living, Corgis are equally suited to city apartments.

GERMAN SHEPHERD
The German Shepherd is the perfect example of why selection of the right breed is so important for would-be owners. Originally known as the Alsatian Wolf Dog, it first appeared at a show in Hanover in 1882. It is a forceful, intelligent dog, ever alert and suspicious of strangers. In the right hands, it is an excellent dog, good-looking, graceful, and handsome.

It is a dominant dog, but if owned by dominant people, it is usually very pleasant to handle. However, to some people who buy dogs as an extension of their own personalities, the German Shepherd represents power and unassailability. For that reason, if this breed gets into the wrong hands, it can be an attacking monster. If you buy a German Shepherd, and you're not a dominant person, obviously the dog will dominate. (Breeds' reputations can be destroyed if the dogs get in the hands of ignorant owners.)

OLD ENGLISH SHEEPDOG
The Old English Sheepdog, which is better known as the shaggy 'Dulux dog' from the paint advertisements, originated in England's West Country, where farmers wanted a dog to herd sheep and drive cattle. Its ancestry probably included the similar-looking Bearded Collie but, despite its English name, European shepherd dogs are also thought to have figured in its evolution. It is a friendly, faithful dog with an intelligent and boisterous manner.

Utility breeds
The utility breeds include the Alaskan Malamute, Boxer, Bullmastiff, Dobermann, Husky, Rottweiler, St Bernard, Samoyed and Schnauzer. The Alaskan Malamute, Husky, Russian Samoyed and the St Bernard are all long-coated dogs bred for working in the cold, northern climates. The St Bernard has become famous for rescuing lost travellers in the Alps, while the Husky, Malamute and Samoyed were originally used by the Eskimos as sled dogs.

ALASKAN MALAMUTE
The Alaskan Malamute derives its name from the Mahlemuts, the Inuit people of upper western Alaska, who used dogs to haul their possessions around on sleds. The dogs, with their gentle, bright eyes and thick coats,

became known for their fortitude and endurance, because of the great distances they would travel.

In recent years the breed has become increasingly popular as a pet and guard dog, but it has proved to be unsuited to the confined spaces of suburbia. Malamutes tend to be one-owner dogs, rather like the Dingo. The dogs are still close to their wild origins and their dominance needs to be carefully controlled. They are currently fashionable, but in many cases owners haven't made an appropriate selection for their lifestyle.

BULLMASTIFF

The Bullmastiff resulted from crossing a Mastiff with a Bulldog, resulting in a quiet, agile tracking dog which was used widely in England to detect poachers. The cross combined the courage and ferocity of the Bulldog with the power, speed and nose of the Mastiff. The Bullmastiff is a big, strong, active dog, and it makes an excellent guard dog and a reliable family pet.

GERMAN BREEDS — BOXER, DOBERMANN, ROTTWEILER AND SCHNAUZER

The Boxer, Dobermann, Rottweiler and Schnauzer are all German breeds. The Boxer resulted late in the 19th century from a cross between a bull-fighting type and a Bulldog; while the Schnauzer, sometimes referred to as the German Terrier, was used as a drovers' dog and watch dog.

The Schnauzer is temperamentally close to a terrier, like the Airedale, which it also resembles. The breed comes in standard and miniature sizes — the miniatures, in particular, make excellent pets.

The Dobermann and Rottweiler are both dominant dogs. The Dobermann was named after Louis Dobermann, who bred the dogs in the late 1800s by crossing the Rottweiler, the German Pinscher, the black-and-tan English Terrier and, possibly, the German Shepherd. The resulting smooth-haired dogs were strong and aggressive and their value was quickly seen as police or army guard dogs. Their temperament is occasionally questioned, but when they are properly trained they are affectionate and obedient.

Similar questions have been posed about the aggression of the Rottweiler, which was originally used as a cattle drover around the town of Rottweil, which was a major European centre for the trading of livestock. Traders accompanying cattle to market used to tie money belts around the necks of the Rottweilers as protection against attack from highwaymen. They were strong-minded, courageous dogs and they required firm discipline. Like the Dobermann, they were often used for guard duties.

People often buy dominant breeds like Rottweilers and German Shepherds as guard dogs, but the best burglar deterrents are small, alert dogs who live in the house and make a lot of noise. Dogs have a sense of possession of their properties when they are secure in their lifestyle, and they will bark the roof off if anyone tries to invade the property.

Intruders will never enter if you have a dog that yaps its head off, so it is not necessary to have a dog that will rip a human limb from limb. The risk of having a dominant dog as a guard dog is that all dominant dogs (unless well controlled and disciplined) make terrible masters. They behave very badly, they're bad-tempered, and they bite. If you feel insecure in our current social climate and decide to buy a Rottweiler to make yourself feel more secure, the dog will become number one, because it will sense your insecurity.

SAMOYED
The fluffy white Samoyed, with its distinctive smiling mouth, was used by the Samoyedes people of Siberia to pull their sleds, herd reindeer and caribou, and to guard them against bears and wolves. The dogs were discovered by fur traders and taken to Europe. They are eager, friendly dogs, and have always loved human company, dating back to the time when they used to share the tents of the Samoyedes people. They are frequent barkers and need a lot of exercise.

Non-sporting dogs
The non-sporting group of dogs is a collection of different breeds with few linking characteristics. They include the Bulldog, Chow Chow, Dalmatian, Great Dane, Poodle, and Shih Tzu.

BULLDOG
Winston Churchill celebrated the Bulldog as a symbol of British determination in the Second World War. They are tough dogs, but fond of humans. They were bred for bull-baiting, to distract the bull long enough for the hunting

party to come up for the kill. The breed now has a lot of genetic faults, including breathing and cardiovascular problems, which have been caused by breeding for appearance, rather than practicality.

CHOW CHOW AND SHIH TZU
The Chow Chow and Shih Tzu are both Chinese dogs. The Chow is also known as the Chinese mutton dog, and was bred from the wild to be eaten. The modern domesticated Chow is not far removed from its wild ancestor, and can be vicious. The Shih Tzu is a tough little dog, like the Pekingese, and it has grown in popularity in recent years.

DALMATIAN AND GREAT DANE
Dalmatians were bred to guard the old mail coaches by running alongside them, so they have a dominant streak. They are high-spirited, and often highly-strung, and need a lot of exercise to burn off their nervous energy. Great Danes were also used as guard dogs, as well as for hunting, and they are classed as giant dogs, often standing one metre tall. In Australia there is currently a high percentage with poor temperaments, and they are not long-lived, generally not surviving beyond six years of age.

POODLE
Poodles continue to vie for the title of the most popular breed, as well as the most intelligent. They were first depicted in European art in the 15th century, and the

breed may have originated in Germany, crossing into France with German troops. Poodles became the rage with the nobility of the 17th and 18th centuries, and were gradually bred to a smaller size. The dogs are highly responsive to their owners, which is one reason why they have become so popular. On top of all that, they are not expensive to keep. They come in standard, miniature and toy sizes.

Consider your temperament and lifestyle

Approximately 200 different breeds of dogs are available in Australia. In making the right selection, what you are trying to do is marry the temperament of the dog with your temperament and lifestyle. It is a bit like a marriage: unless you are compatible, problems can arise, which is very wearing on the spirit. However, unlike humans, dogs don't change their minds or attachments. In all our dealings with humans, there is always that element of doubt, but dogs are always consistent, and they can always be trusted. Even an ill-tempered and badly-behaved dog is always consistent and welcoming, and the same can't be said of all human beings.

In the same way that Australian dogs resulted from breeders' efforts to fuse certain instincts and characteristics, so other countries bred dogs with specific characteristics to carry out their own special tasks. With the exception of the toys, which were produced as lapdogs and household companions, none of the breeds was intended to sit alone in a backyard, with nothing to do. Dogs were given noses to sniff, eyes to detect movement, courage to see off hostile animals and intruders, brains to work out problems, and bodies to chase and retrieve. Even though we buy them as pets, and we don't want them to go out hunting and chasing, the original instincts of the dog still remain.

We must always remember these basic instincts, and the diverse needs of the different breeds, which need to be met through providing the dog with adequate security, activity and entertainment. If you fail to acknowledge them you will get behaviour problems, which are really no more than the animal trying to be itself.

Dogs have a very simple attitude to life: they want to love and obey the boss dog and, in exchange, the boss dog must supply security and certainty. If you do that, and select the right dog, you have got a true companion, and you will derive nothing but pleasure from the relationship. You have found the perfect canine partner.

THE PUPPY COMES HOME

It's no good going to the pet shop one Saturday morning, falling in love with a puppy and bringing it home at lunchtime without any infrastructure to support it. Before the dog gets to the house you need to have a basket or kennel, food and water bowls, a suitable lead and collar, grooming equipment, and secure fences round the property, to make sure it is escape-proof. Once the puppy is home, allow it free range of the back yard, so that it imprints the area in its memory, and gets to know that this is its territory. Right from the time you get it home at eight weeks old it is responding to the environment and learning.

Be boss dog from the start

From day one establish who's boss dog. Put a collar on the dog to carry its identification, but also to give you control of its head. From the first minute home, the puppy must be exposed to an unchanging set of rules, about when and where it eats, where it sleeps, and how it is house-trained. Once you have established the rules, stick to them, because dogs need consistency and a regular rhythm to their lives. They are very close observers and they quickly learn these patterns.

The majority of puppies under 12 weeks of age are introverts. Leaving their mother is a shock, so initially they can be quite timid, but they soon realise that there's so much to learn and do. Around 12 weeks the average puppy will clearly believe it is master of its environment, and it will become quite bold and extroverted. This coincides with the peak of their learning curve, and while the puppy should be encouraged to form its own character, you've got to recognise all challenges to your authority, or the race will quickly be lost — even at this tender age.

Everything taught to your puppy between eight and 18 weeks, or everything that you fail to teach, is permanently learnt. After five months it becomes increasingly difficult to get lessons across to a puppy in a short period of time, and from nine months you need absolute patience to educate a dog and a determination never to give up, even though you may have repeated the lesson to the point of despair.

If you take on a pre-owned dog, you will come to understand how difficult it is to eradicate things that were learnt from the former owner, or to introduce things that were not taught. You should understand that you are taking on unexplained behaviour which has everything to do with the previous owner. If the owner did a good job training the dog, all well and good, but if the person allowed the dog free rein, that's when you can get trouble. The older the dog is, the harder it is to correct its behaviour.

Puppies only learn by experience, and that experience is either pleasant or unpleasant. So you must use a pleasant reward or scolding to teach the animal. If your dog is doing all the things you want it to do, it should receive pleasure, through praise and patting, or an edible reward like a bone or a reward biscuit. You must never forget to praise a job well done.

When you go to pat the dog, you should start by patting its back or chest, and then work up towards its head. It is very threatening to a dog to have an outstretched hand coming towards its head. Dogs also like to be ruffled around the sides of their head and ears, as it simulates their mother's licking, which can be quite rough.

If the dog is not doing what you want, scold it, through the tone of your voice, by a light tap to the bridge of the nose or with the flat of the hand on the rump. A reinforcing light smack, if it follows a scolding, is all right when the dog is young, but you should have the dog under voice control early on. If you have to hit your dog aggressively, you are admitting that you haven't got the dog under control. Punishment procedures in dog training have a limited and specific place because the lessons are not willingly learnt if accompanied by punishment, and there is the potential for cruelty.

It is normal for a puppy to play bite, including on human hands, which it will take in its mouth. This 'mouthing' is instinctive behaviour, and something the puppy will grow out of, but it may still need some correction so that it does not become a permanent feature. A puppy cannot know that mouthing hurts, unless you teach it that it's unacceptable. If it continues biting, the animal should be growled at, harshly.

A word of warning: if you are introducing a new dog to a home with an existing dog which has not been trained properly, you run the risk of having two badly behaved dogs on your hands, because the new one will model itself on the old one.

House-training

When you house-train, select an area of the garden where it is acceptable for the dog to urinate and defecate. You must decide this when you bring the puppy home. A young puppy will use its bladder every half hour or so, and it should not be left inside for longer than 30 minutes. Take the dog out, and praise it when it does something, and that way the dog learns very quickly that the 'boss dog' is immensely pleased when it urinates and defecates in the one place.

Always supervise the puppy when it eats, and as soon as it has finished, take it outside. If you devote yourself to all of this early on, you will get the message across to the puppy quite quickly, and the length of time it takes to house-train the dog will be shortened considerably. But never think that your puppy is reliably watertight under nine months.

Puppies cannot rationalise, and they cannot connect scolding with urinating unless it's done while the puppy is urinating. If you find a puddle half an hour after the puppy has urinated, and then rub the dog's nose in it, the puppy is not going to understand why you're doing this. The scolding has to be done while the dog is in the act of performing the undesirable action.

Puppies will not easily wet or foul their bedding, so one of the quickest ways to make the puppy hang on is to confine it overnight in a transport cage for six to eight hours. The pup should be taken outside to 'empty out' last thing before you retire, and do not give it a drink just before or during confinement. The cage should be just big enough to allow the puppy to stand up, turn around, and lie flat, with a slight amount of room for growth. You might have to allow for a couple of changes of cage during the house-training period, to allow for the puppy's growth.

In some people's minds, caging anything is cruel, but you're only talking about leaving the puppy in the cage overnight while it's asleep. During the day the puppy should be out and about in the back yard. You can use stakes and chicken wire to construct a puppy pen so the dog doesn't wander too far. The pen should enclose a kennel which will shelter the animal from the elements. Wherever possible, the kennel should be sited near to the house and as close as possible to the major exit door, and certainly within hearing range of the most lived-in room, which is usually the kitchen. That way the dog can retain some reference to the 'boss dog', and the other inhabitants.

Sleeping arrangements

Like the overnight cage used for house-training, the kennel should be big enough to allow the dog to stand up and turn around, 'nest' with its paws and lie flat. Dogs, unlike humans, do not sleep right through the night, and often they will wake up in the early morning and move around, or change their sleeping positions. Dogs who sleep outside may go roaming in the middle of the night, but when you wake them in the morning they will be back in the kennel as though nothing has happened.

You must make the decision about whether the dog will sleep inside or outside the day it comes home, and stick to it. If you allow the dog to sleep inside as a young puppy, it will always want to sleep inside, and it will cry and perform if you suddenly decide to put it outside. The animal that sleeps inside enjoys protection from the weather, makes the perfect watch dog, and is not distracted by possums or any of the other things that go bump in the night, that might cause it to bark if it's outside. But if your dog is to sleep inside, it needs to be well-trained to respect furniture, and to accept confinement for long periods, and this may include denial of access to some parts of the house. If you remain concerned about soiling accidents then have a 'doggy door' commercially fitted in an external house door to allow the dog an emergency exit to a well-fenced area within the backyard.

It's important to give your dog a properly designed area in which to sleep. Its basket or sleeping area should contain warm bedding, which can be made of fabric or newspaper. The drawback to using fabric is that flea eggs can remain in the weave of the material, but this doesn't usually happen with shredded newspaper. You must wash fabric bedding weekly in the flea season to keep it free from flea eggs. Newspaper bedding is easier because it can be thrown away and replaced each week. Dogs should be taught the discipline of having their own sleeping arrangements, and I'm not in favour of them sleeping on furniture or beds, because they bring in dirt and fleas from outside.

Bathing and grooming

You should bath your dog when required, with a soap or shampoo specifically designed for dogs, as human soaps are too strong and can cause dermatitis. I recommend that if your dog has a skin problem, you should select a medicated soap or shampoo that has been designed specifically to help that problem. You will find that large numbers of dogs who love swimming and splashing in the dirtiest duck pond will hate to be bathed, because bathing is owner-inflicted and not done by free choice. Dogs' general attitude to water depends on how they've been introduced to it. It's very frightening to some of them, and they need to be introduced gently. Some dogs will never accept it. When bathing a dog or allowing it to swim, always check to see that water has not entered the ear canals as moisture sets up a perfect environment for fungal ear infections. Drying drops are available from your vet. I automatically dose my dogs after a bath or a swim to make sure their ears are dry.

Grooming should begin as soon as you get a dog. If it has a long coat it should be brushed every day, but you can reduce this to every other day if your dog is short-haired. It usually takes eight to 10 minutes to groom a dog properly. You need to use a sturdy comb with metal teeth to separate old, dead hair from the new hair, and a firm bristled brush, or a rubber-toothed grooming device to get rid of dirt or scurf and to tone up the skin.

If you don't brush your dog, its coat will become dirty and parasites will have a protected home, which in turn leads to skin irritation and dermatitis. Dead hair also forms fur knots with the live hair, and this is a further source of irritation to the skin. Dogs that aren't groomed have duller coats, and they become unkempt and moth-eaten in appearance.

Dogs will moult twice a year, usually around late March and late October. This is a natural shedding of the coat, usually heralding the thinning of the coat for summer, or its thickening for winter. The moult is triggered by a change in the daylight hours, either an increase following winter, or a decrease, after summer.

Moulting is most obvious on double-coated dogs like the Labrador, Golden Retriever, German Shepherd and Corgi, but it will hardly be noticed on the short-haired, smooth-coated breeds. The length of the moult varies from six to eight weeks, and it will depend on how much time the owner spends brushing the dog. If the dog is vigorously groomed on a daily basis, the moulting time will decrease. Moulting is a deliberate shedding and renewal of the coat, and it can't be done by the dog alone; the process must be helped along by the owner. If the dog fails to drop its coat, the dead hair will ball up, trapping the live hair and irritating the skin. The coat will also look bedraggled.

Vaccinations

Puppies should have had their first vaccination between six and eight weeks, to guard against distemper, hepatitis and parvovirus. All are viral diseases and are all generally fatal. Distemper affects the nervous system, and particularly, brain cells and the gut. Hepatitis affects the liver cells, and parvovirus mainly affects the cells lining the gastrointestinal tract, causing violent vomiting and diarrhoea. The second vaccination should be done between 12 and 14 weeks and, depending on the particular type of parvovirus vaccine used, a third vaccination may be necessary between 16 and 18 weeks. A vaccination can also be given to protect your puppy against kennel cough, which is the canine equivalent of the common cold.

Puppies should also begin taking tablets to protect them against heartworm by the time they're three months old. The worm can grow up to 30 centimetres long and destroys the right-side chamber of the heart. If untreated, it can cause heart failure. Tablets to prevent heartworm can be taken either daily or monthly. Worming tablets to protect puppies against roundworm and the other worms affecting the bowel should be started at two to three weeks of age.

Diet

The link between a poor diet, disease and a short life is well established. It is important to ensure that your new pup is placed on a good diet from day one of ownership and that this diet is varied to meet the nutritional requirements of each life-stage.

The most common illness in puppies is gastrointestinal upsets, which cause diarrhoea and vomiting. Despite these symptoms, they usually remain bright. These upsets usually occur because the dog is given the wrong food — often milk — or because the transition from the breeder's diet to the home diet has been made too quickly. Dogs will drink milk because it's meat-flavoured, but most dogs cannot digest milk lactose (which is a milk sugar) because they lack the necessary liver enzyme. As a result, the undigested lactose causes a reaction in the lining of the colon. If your dog has a food-induced diarrhoea, quickly put it on a non-allergenic diet of white meats, vegetables and rice. You can also give it plenty of water. The diarrhoea should cease within 24 hours. Seek veterinary advice if it doesn't.

Puppies need a diet that will promote growth and good health, and which contains the five essential ingredients — protein, carbohydrate, fat, vitamins and minerals. Protein comes from red and white meat, fish, and the occasional egg. Carbohydrates are contained in cereals, grains, pasta, potatoes and rice. Fat, which is needed to maintain the dog's coat and supply the fat-soluble vitamins A, D, and E, should make up about 5 per cent of the diet, and can come from cod liver oil or vegetable oil, as well as the fat from meat. The water-soluble vitamins B and C come from vegetables. Some minerals occur naturally in meat and vegetables, but if a dog is on a natural diet, we generally recommend that the animal is given a mineral supplement. Large dogs should also be given a mineral supplement while they are growing.

When your puppy first comes home it should be fed little and often, at breakfast, lunch and dinner. As it grows, it will start to lose interest in the midday meal, and it should be restricted to two meals a day, in the morning and evening. A dog requires a varied diet, consisting of natural foods as well as the commercially prepared canned and dry foods. The more variety in the diet, the better it is for the dog. If you feed your dog a natural diet it's important to ensure that it receives the right balance of ingredients, with greens as well as meat and water. If the dog starts wanting to eat grass, this indicates that it needs more green vegetables in its diet.

COMMERCIAL FOODS

However much we would prefer to feed dogs a natural diet, the fact is that preparing such food is quite complicated. Not only is it difficult to ensure that we get the balance of the five basic ingredients correct for the particular age of the dog, but we need a fair amount of time available each day to purchase the raw ingredients and prepare the food. It is therefore little wonder that many dog owners prefer to feed their dogs a commercially prepared food. Nonetheless, the Australian Companion Animal Report 2010 (found on the Australian Companion Animal Council's website) determined that while commercial dog food sales grew by 2.6 per cent in the year 2009, half of all pet dogs were still fed food prepared in the home.

When considering which type of commercial food to purchase it is important to refer to the manufacturer's claims for their product. Canned food and semi-moist food is not a complete diet and requires supplementing with commercial dry food or natural ingredients. Premium dry food is a complete diet and can be fed as the sole source of nutrition. I have raised many dogs now on premium dry food and have found them to have lived long, healthy, active lives.

Many dog owners insist that dogs should be fed raw or cooked meat misunderstanding that meat protein is contained in commercial dry food.

Dogs are occasionally intolerant of some ingredients in canned food and the result can be vomiting, diarrhoea, or, more commonly, flatulence, caused by allergic colitis. This often occurs in the older dog. If your dog develops an allergy to certain types of food ask your vet for guidance on feeding a non-allergenic diet.

THE IMPORTANCE OF BONES

Raw meaty bones should be incorporated into a dog's diet from day one, and they should be given to the animal at least three times a week. For years I was criticised by many of my veterinary colleagues for advocating the eating of bones, but I think it's now generally accepted that dogs must have bones to chew on. This was confirmed in a report commissioned by the Australian Veterinary Association and published in the October 1994 edition of the Australian Veterinary Journal, which recommended supplementing dogs' diets with raw bones to prevent gum disease. The article, by Professor A D J Watson, from the Department of Veterinary Clinical Sciences at the University of Sydney, found that dogs eating soft food were more likely to contract gum disease, and that the inclusion of hard food, such as large dog biscuits, rawhide, or oxtail helped keep the gums healthier.

Professor Watson recommended that the diet for dogs (and cats) should have physical qualities, including texture, abrasiveness and 'chewiness', that would help control plaque and maintain oral health. He said that raw, meaty bones should be given to dogs at least once a week, and preferably two or three times.

In practice, you can always tell the dogs that eat bones by their healthy teeth and gums. If a dog is not allowed to chew and gnaw on hard substances, there is a build-up of tartar on the dog's teeth, and this causes inflammation of the gums. Where you have inflammation, you have tooth decay, and where you have decay, you have bacteria and pus. If bacteria gains access to the blood system via the gums it can result in damage to the lining of the heart, and to the kidney and liver.

The essential part of the exercise is that a dog should spend time gnawing. Bones that the dog crunches and eats straight away, like chicken bones, do less good than beef or lamb bones which the dog will spend a longer time gnawing or chewing. Despite the caution from some veterinary circles, I have found it safe to give a dog any kind of beef, lamb or chicken bone (provided it is a proper leg bone from the chicken, and not one of the small, spiky bones), and I'm still waiting to see my first case of penetration of the bowel by a bone. There will be the odd dog who has trouble with bones, but this does not mean bones are not an essential ingredient. If your dog vomits pieces of bone or passes them in its stool you should not continue to feed it bones.

Walking your puppy

Once a puppy has had its first vaccination, and the injection has had the chance to work, which normally takes eight to 10 days, it can go for a walk. Don't try to put a lead on until the dog is used to its collar. A dog will have a temper tantrum when you put a collar on for the first time, and another tantrum when you put on the lead, and when you first tie it up, but they are valuable lessons, and all reinforce that you are the boss dog. Each subsequent time you put the dog on its lead you are repeating the lesson. A dog should always learn to be tied up, even though you don't intend to do that most of the time because, in an emergency, it's the only reliable way of restraining it.

Puppy classes

Puppy classes are just as important for dogs as kindergarten is for children, and you should start them at 12 weeks, after the second vaccination. The classes help them to socialise, and when you progress on to proper obedience lessons, which are mainly concerned with teaching the owner how to control their dog the dog will be more prepared. Where an owner is not the boss dog, the obedience classes help the person to learn how to assert themselves with their dog. They also teach the owner how to exert the authority of the boss dog through voice control, by using the basic commands like 'sit', 'stay', and 'come'. For the average pet owner, this is sufficient, and can be taught to the dog in six to 12 months, but if you want to go on, obedience classes can be great fun, and achievement gives a great boost to the owner's ego.

The period from three to nine months of age coincides

with a very rapid growing phase in your dog, and you can usually see this from the spirit of youthful enthusiasm it has. They've come to terms with their environment, and think they know all there is to know, with the result being that the average puppy will be quite cocky. There will be frequent challenges to the boss dog, as they explore the physical boundaries around them, as well as the development of their relationship with the boss dog. They desperately need guidance during this period.

By 12 months small and medium dogs are physically and mentally mature, whereas the larger breeds, from the Labrador upwards, are physically mature at one year, but they will not be mentally mature until they're about three. The mature dog has learned from experience, and it knows all about its environment.

All this, of course, presupposes that the dog has been in a training routine since it came home as an eight-week-old puppy. If this hasn't happened, you'll end up with a behavioural ratbag which the owner grows to dislike more and more. Commonly 10 to 12 months is the time when people get fed up with a dog and dump it, or leave it with the RSPCA.

The first 12–18 months will require a large input of guidance and discipline from the owner. After 18 months, if you've been consistent in setting the rules, the work begins to pay off. By the age of three you should have reached the stage where the dog will anticipate what will please you, and correction will only be occasional. The well-trained dog will have learned to follow the boss dog, and live by the rules.

2

Behaviour

BOSS DOGS AND BEHAVIOUR PROBLEMS

There's no secret why my dogs are well-behaved — because I'm the boss. Rule number one of dog ownership is that dogs must have a boss. In the wild, dogs are pack animals, and they have a leader, so in the domestic situation, the owner must become the pack leader. Dogs love to follow a leader, and they're not meant to be 'boss dogs' unless they are in the wild.

Rule number two is that the boss dog sets the parameters of behaviour. If the owner tries to run a partnership with the dog, the dog doesn't understand that. The reason people have unruly dogs is that the dog has been allowed to become the boss dog. Owners have to keep reasserting who's boss.

Male dogs who have not been desexed are more likely to be boss dogs than females, but I have seen plenty of dominant bitches. About 15 per cent of the animals I see are boss dogs, and the animal's size has little bearing on its desire for dominance. A high number of lapdogs write their own tickets. One of the most savage dogs I've encountered was a Chihuahua. The Rottweiler weighs at least 40 kilos and takes some stopping but, because of its smallness, the Chihuahua can at least be managed.

The vet who had the practice before me used to say, 'Never trust a Chow.' They're mercurial, highly dominant dogs. When I voiced this opinion at a dog club, a Chow breeder stood up and said it was rubbish. I replied, 'One day you'll see what I mean.' The following week at a show the breeder was attacked by his own Chow in the ring. The next time I went to the dog club, the owner still had his arm swathed in bandages, and he required plastic surgery.

The most common boss dog is the one who has its way, regardless of the owner. Everything is fine until you try to correct the dog. He will sit on your favourite chair, and if you try to move him, he'll bite you. Dogs will also bolster their control by 'food fadding' — refusing to eat the food put in front of them. By not eating the food, they engender panic in the owner, who rushes out to buy different kinds of food, which produce the same response from the dog. They exercise this quite subtle control over their owner via the dinner plate.

The owner usually says, 'I love him, even though he's naughty,' and has all kinds of excuses for allowing the bad behaviour to go on. It is a simple case of the dog being allowed to exert authority. The dog is perfectly behaved as long as you never do anything to control it, but the minute it has to submit to something in the vet's surgery, the problem shows up. Owners try to explain away the dog's dominance by saying the dog is nervous, after being frightened by a particular experience, often with a vet. They claim the dog has never been the same since something you, or someone else, did to him. No-one ever says, 'The dog is biting to show his dominance, and I let him get that way.' The problem stems from the fact that the owner has never taken control.

Is your dog a boss dog?

The mark of whether a dog is a boss dog is how it behaves outside the family. Boss dogs still want to be dominant when they are brought in to me at the surgery. When the dog snarls, the owner thinks it is because the dog doesn't like vets, but it is because the dog is dominant. Most people won't accept that their dog has become a boss dog, because it is a reflection on their failure to put the dog in its place. When I examine the dog, and he or she snarls, it is not because I'm a vet, but because I'm taking excessive liberties and he or she is saying, 'I'm the boss dog, how dare you touch me!'

A woman came to the surgery once with a Blue Heeler. Before I did anything, she said, 'I'd better put a muzzle on him, he doesn't like you.' She put the muzzle on, and when I went to touch the dog its eyes bulged, and it rumbled and growled. The woman said, 'Butch, don't be silly,' but Butch didn't give a damn. He was determined I wouldn't touch him. Every boss dog will get ill one day, and someone has to handle them. The vet is supposed to be like Mandrake the Magician, gesturing hypnotically at the dog, which suddenly melts. When Butch was brought home at eight weeks, he should have been clearly told who was boss. Owners try to rationalise their dog's behaviour, or give excuses for it. It's the phase of the moon, or the hot weather, or the cold weather — everything except the truth.

A woman came to see me with a young Cocker Spaniel that had a problem in its mouth. When I went to examine the dog, it tried to bite me, and the woman explained it had been acting aggressively since it went to the clipper's. I asked whether it was a boss dog. 'Oh, yes,' she said, 'he's always been like that.' When I suggested that she should assert herself more, she replied, 'But I'm a cat lady, Dr Wirth.'

Dogs don't respond to being treated like cats. The woman had taken on her daughter's dog, even though she didn't like dogs. She was treating the dog like a cat, and the dog was in charge. It was a classic case of someone being dumped with a dog they didn't like and couldn't control.

I've had other dogs come into the surgery that are so aggressive that neither I nor the owner could control the animal. One young male brought in a Rottweiler to be desexed. The owner had the dog on a long piece of rope, but no-one could get within a bull's roar of it. If anyone went near him, he went to eat them. Other clients in the waiting room were terrified, and standing up on the benches. When we asked the owner to reel the dog in he said he couldn't, because he was frightened of it. We couldn't handle the dog, so we suggested the owner take it away, get some control over it, and then we'd desex it. We never saw him again.

On another occasion an owner brought in a Cattle Dog with a broken leg. He had been hit by a car. We sedated the dog, but 24 hours later, when the shock and sedation had worn off, we were confronted by a savage dog. We told the owner we couldn't handle the dog, and sent him down to the kennels. The dog greeted him with a resounding bite, and his immediate response was to demand that we destroy the dog. I pointed out that I would have difficulty handling the dog to destroy it. 'I don't care,' he said, 'I don't want to see it again.' He walked out of the surgery, leaving us with a raging dog in the kennels and instructions to kill it — if we could get near it.

Some clients keep getting boss dogs, and as soon as they lose an animal they come back with one just as bad. More boss dogs seem to be owned by women, perhaps because women are often reluctant to be assertive with the dog. I've even known situations where the husband can't get in to bed with his wife because the dog is on the bed, and threatens to bite the husband when he gets in. It fascinates me that in some cases the woman does nothing to retrieve the situation.

THE EFFECT OF NEGLECT

Sometimes a dog's dominance can stem from the owner's neglect and failure to train the dog or correct its behaviour early in the dog's life. I remember being called to deal with a savage Kelpie who was fenced in the backyard. If anyone came near him he became madder and madder. The owner called me to the house because the dog was too violent to bring into the surgery. When I got there the dog snarled and threw itself at the fence. I asked the man how he fed the dog. 'I throw food out of the window,' he said. Why did he keep the dog? 'Because I love him,' he answered.

I suggested we put the dog down, but we couldn't get near him. I carry a stick with a lasso on it, for catching recalcitrant dogs, and eventually we were able to get the lasso around the dog's head and pin it down long enough for me to give it an injection. The dog was seven, and he'd been desexed, but it made no difference. He had inherited aggression, which worsened with age. Even the worst temperament can be modified if you get to the dog when it's young, but this owner had no control and he was clearly terrified of the dog.

This is an extreme example of a boss dog, and the owner had only compounded the dog's existing problems. Initially the man had bought an unsatisfactory dog, which proved too much for him. His answer was not to dump the dog, but ignore it, and then he covered that by saying he loved the animal. Instead of seeking guidance on the dog he simply left it in the backyard, and the animal went from bad to worse.

People get sick of their dog's uncorrected behaviour, but the owners are part of the problem. Often people who have difficulty asserting themselves in daily life tend to choose assertive dogs. Then you get the owner saying the dog has a behaviour problem.

DESEXING

Having a dog desexed may also help to curb its dominance. People think that desexing is done solely to stop reproduction, but it also removes the secondary sex characteristics, such as aggression, assertiveness and wanting to get out to mate, which all result from the male hormone. One client was very upset about the abnormal sexual behaviour of her Jack Russell: it was dominant, used to bite people, and tried to mount everything in sight, including human legs and the cat. We desexed the dog and the problems disappeared.

Dogs are very aware of the pecking order within a family. I've known cases where a dominant dog will struggle with the youngest child to make sure it doesn't get pushed into the bottom spot in the social order. Whenever the child tries to assert him or herself, the dog will try to put them back into bottom place. If the child is more assertive, they will be challenged by the dog, but will eventually topple it. Dogs will never threaten you if you're the boss, but if the dog has reached the stage of believing it is the boss, then you've got problems.

OWNER ASSERTION

Allowing the animal to become a boss dog is the primary reason for behaviour problems in dogs. The second reason is that the dog's instinctive behaviour has never been modified by the owner. When dogs dig up plants, rip down the washing, or piddle in the house, they're just being dogs, but you have to modify that behaviour by teaching your dog to look after the house and the garden.

Dogs will also behave according to their breed characteristics. An owner may think their dog has a behavioural problem if it chases cars, but generally the dogs that chase cars are those that were bred to chase, like Border Collies and Kelpies. Kelpies are bred to react to movement, and it is a corruption of a natural instinct for them to chase cars, rather than sheep or cattle. Modify the behaviour and fence the dog in, so it doesn't get run over chasing cars.

Start teaching a dog when it is young. If a puppy does something wrong in your presence, like digging a hole in the garden, smack it lightly over the bridge of the nose, or on the rump with an open hand. This simulates the mother's bite. A mother will growl if she doesn't like what the puppy is doing. Then she nips, to reinforce the message. Adapt this technique, and the dog will soon understand when you are angry. Your growl means what their mother's did — that you'll act if they don't do what you want them to. You should progress rapidly from smacking to using voice control.

The minute a puppy is brought home at eight weeks, apply pressure so that it knows who is boss dog. The puppy should know the rules before it is six months old, and those rules should be kept, because dogs need consistency. If you don't set the rules early in your relationship, you'll spend many years repenting.

Dog temperaments

A dog's temperament becomes extroverted at about 12 weeks of age, and it will show the dog's tendency to be dominant, aggressive or fearful. You must treat fearful dogs with extreme patience and encouragement, and let them know that you, the 'boss dog', are supportive. Unless you're the 'boss dog', you can't help the dog overcome its fear. Socialisation may help, but if the animal is fearful of humans, or other dogs, you must expose it regularly to that fear, and through familiarity, it will gradually lose that fearfulness.

Like humans, some dogs are born with a bad temperament, and they can be identified almost immediately. While owners can often get the animal to behave for them, in many cases the dogs won't be handled by anyone else. One sign of this poor temperament is 'fear aggression', where the dog will show its fear in threatening situations by becoming excessively aggressive. Because the dog is in fear, and you persist in frightening it, it will bite you.

Fear-aggressive dogs respond badly to a situation they're unhappy about. When the dog is scared, it will excite the 'fight-or-flight' syndrome, and the dog will either stand its ground and defend itself, or it will run away. You must work out which situations frighten the dog, and gradually try to modify the behaviour. It takes a great deal of patience to help the dog to learn that there are more dogs than itself, and more humans than its owner. The earlier you start this desensitisation, the better the result. Sometimes children aggravate the dog's fear, and risk being bitten, but parents must warn their children about handling dogs. A good parent will train the family dog, and also educate their children about what to expect from the dog.

Some fearful dogs cling to the owner's lead for security, and become frightened when the lead is taken off. Again, you must try and build the dog's confidence by removing the lead when there is no-one else in the park. Encourage the dog to explore, while keeping its eye attuned to you.

BARKING

Many so-called behavioural faults in dogs are no different from those found in children. They all like attention, and they need to be noticed by the leader. Barking is a dog's way of communicating that it is happy, disturbed or wary.

The greatest number of dog complaints to local councils involve barking. The electronic collar, which costs around $300, has been proposed as a high-tech way of stopping dogs barking. It is claimed that the collar works by giving the dog a shock each time it barks, or by releasing an unpleasant odour. I have found that the collars fail to work because the central ingredient is missing, namely leadership from the 'boss dog' to fix the cause of the barking. People are trying to overcome their failure to train their dog by using some 'whizz-bang' electronic device. In some cases the devices temporaily stop the dog barking, but many animals don't react, or they cease for a while, then start again. You cannot teach a dog by excessive aversion therapy and there is also the issue of cruelty, with many states banning their use.

Ultimately the collars won't work because they don't follow dogs' instinctive manner of learning, which is to take leadership from the boss dog. Dogs still possess the same make-up they've always had, and you defy a dog's behavioural instincts at your own peril.

Dogs need to be taught about barking at a very early age. From day one, every time your dog barks, investigate why it is barking. If it is barking for no apparent reason, you should scold it. You must make it clear that it is not acceptable for the dog to bark at possums at 3 am. The dog will quickly learn when not to bark. At the same time dogs need to be allowed to be dogs, and that includes barking when something strange upsets them. If my dogs bark in the middle of the night I get up and investigate the cause straight away.

Dogs have a wider hearing range than humans, and they pick up higher pitches than we do. Some dogs are frightened by sudden noises which is called being 'gun-shy'. Others will suddenly howl at a particular noise, and it is often because the noise simulates the pack leader's howl, which calls them to rally. The howl is an instinctive reaction to the pack leader's call.

Barking at the garbos, or unusual noises like planes in the sky, is reasonable dog behaviour, and not a behavioural problem. Dogs are territorial animals, and when the garbos come along once a week, they think, 'How dare these people come through our territory like that, making all this noisy crashing and bashing. We don't crash and bash.' So the dogs bark, and kick up a fuss. No territorial dog will enjoy a loud incursion into its territory, and will protest.

We confine the dog to a quarter-acre block, but its territory is two or three times bigger than that. It can encompass neighbours' property, and the public area in front of the house. It also includes aerial territory, so if you have low-flying aircraft, or possums in the trees, they are seen as invaders, and foreign to the environment. The dog will bark to alert the invader that they have been sighted, and to warn the members of the pack within the invaded territory.

Dogs will protect their territory by barking at people who come to the front door, or at people or dogs outside the car, which is an extension of their territory. A dog can be in a car and it starts barking when it sees an owner walking their dog, because it sees the other dog as invading its space, and the pack has to be told. Behavioural problems arise when a dog continues to bark, long after the invasion of its territory has ceased.

Dogs will also bark in response to noisy space invaders, such as motor bikes or big trucks. My dogs used to bark at the noise of a nail gun being used to build the house across the road, because it was an abnormal noise invading their territory. They also respond to the ambulance and police sirens, which simulates the pack leader's call, by yodelling back.

All these are manifestations of normal dog behaviour that need to be modified in an urban environment. When someone knocks at the door, a dog will look to the 'boss dog' for leadership, and the 'boss dog' has to say, 'It's all right, you can be quiet.' If the dog goes on barking in that situation, it doesn't have a behaviour problem; the owner does. The owner has failed to modify the dog's behaviour by imprinting on it that he is the 'boss dog'; the one who determines whether there is a threat.

Owners never think behavioural problems are their fault. Take dogs who bark if they're left at home on their own during the day. If the pack leader disappears for 12 hours, of course the dog gets upset, and starts howling and barking. The dog is behaving normally, but that behaviour hasn't been modified to suit the quarter-acre block, and the owner's expectations.

I get a lot of people saying they can't stand their dog barking. Incessant barking, barking at imaginary things or at things the dog is used to, is a behaviour problem, and should have been modified. You can teach a dog to do anything if you have the will to do so. We educate our children, but none of us seem to believe we have to do something similar with our dogs. Some owners see dogs as a chattel, and think they will magically do what they're supposed to, regardless of instinct. They see dogs as an appendage which you take off and on, like a sports coat. The truth about dog ownership is that you have to meet your dog halfway. It is not just a matter of providing food, water and a bed.

SEPARATION ANXIETY

Of all the animals domesticated by humans, dogs are the most dependent on us. If you bring a puppy into the house and make it dependent on you, the moment the umbilical cord is cut it will become distressed. This is the cause of the separation anxiety that many dogs feel when their owner goes away. But there are individual variations in dogs, just as there are in children, and some dogs have the opposite problem — they have not been encouraged to bond with their owners and exhibit a strong streak of independence.

Between 15 and 20 per cent of dogs experience separation anxiety. The dog's principal concern is to find you, the owner. It vocalises its distress by putting out a call to you, by either barking or howling. Some dogs may become anxious if you leave them outside when you go inside and will do anything to be with you. Other dogs will get out and go looking for you when you leave the property, which is why I tell people not to leave their dog in the backyard when they go away on holiday — it can slip out when the neighbour comes in to feed it.

The older the dog is when the decision is made to correct the problem, the harder it is to do. You have to teach a dog that you will disappear, but you will also return. The first thing is to ensure you have help. You have to find someone, a friend or relative, who will go and identify the behaviour, and correct it immediately. The dog must be disciplined in the act of howling or barking. No discipline meted out afterwards ever works. You, or friends or relatives, have to give a scolding which the dog realises is a significant rebuff to its behaviour.

It's also important that you don't make a big production out of leaving your dog. Sometimes separation anxiety is made worse by the boss dog encouraging dependency, so don't draw attention to the fact that you are going.

If a dog is persistently getting out of a property to go and find its owner, it may be necessary to put the dog in a pen. These can cost around $1500, but if you know your dog has separation anxiety, and will do anything to get out to try to find you, then $1500 is not a lot to spend. A pen may also be the best answer for those 'Houdini' dogs who are always getting out and committing social indiscretions.

Dogs will try to pay you back if they're upset with you for doing something without them, or leaving them alone for a while. Dogs left in the backyard on their own often get upset, and when you get home you may be confronted by deliberate wreckage, just to let you know your actions haven't gone unnoticed. The usual 'paybacks' are to chew something, like a plant or a piece of furniture, or to dig a hole. The hole dug in the garden is the dog's 'payback' for your getting home an hour later than usual. Dogs are creatures of habit, and if there is a variation to that habit they get upset and respond very quickly.

Dogs can also become upset if they are suddenly displaced in the family by the arrival of a new member or another dog. The established animal has been closely bonded and there is an expectation built into that bonding. Suddenly the bonding is broken by the arrival of a new animal, a baby, partner or elderly relative, and the dog can respond by seeking attention, to try to restore the expectations. The owner must ensure that the new arrival does not reduce the amount of affection or attention given to the dog.

DOGS AND BOREDOM

Apart from being educated about the rules of the household, dogs also need to be amused. Boredom is the cause of many holes dug in the garden or washing ripped from the line — the devil finds work for idle paws. Most young dogs are mentally highly active, and if you don't occupy them, the trouble begins. It doesn't take long for the average dog to investigate the garden and learn where everything is, and after a few months the environment presents no fresh challenges. If you haven't made your dog's life interesting, the animal will find its own ways of amusing itself.

You've got to spend time with your dog, even if it is with simple communication, reinforcing the message that you are boss dog. You must give it a taste of adventure, by taking it into the wider environment, and that means regularly walking your dog. Breeds like Labradors and Kelpies need to walk five kilometres a day, so, if you can't walk the dog, find someone to do it for you. The walk burns up physical energy, and some of that inherent curiosity. If you bring the dog home from a walk and give it a bone, this will occupy it mentally. After that it will snooze instead of digging up the lawn.

Dogs are very predictable in their behaviour, and they will always react in a set order. If you walk up to Sheelagh, my Irish Terrier, in the street and she growls, she's saying, 'I don't like you, strange dog, and if you continue to approach me, I'm going to take sterner action.' A growl warns you that a dog may bite. Once the dog has curled its upper lip, it will bite without further notice. If the human ignores these warning signs, and suffers a bite as a result of their actions, it is always the dog that takes the blame, even though the human was at fault for not recognising the dog's behaviour, and taking suitable precautions.

People often ring me up and say that their dog has got a behaviour problem. But what they've really got is a human behaviour problem. The human has destroyed the dog's pack, and the dog has learned to accept the human as surrogate family. But, in return, the human has not learned to understand or modify the dog's behaviour.

HAPPY DOGS

The dawning of each new day finds a dog rested, refreshed, raring to go, and looking to the boss dog for guidance. The perfect response is to take it for a walk, because a dog is at its most energetic first thing, so it's always good to walk then, and afterwards get them to eat a bone. The key is that you must stick to whatever routine you establish.

Dogs like games and doing things, whether it's chasing balls and sticks, and bringing them back, or leaping after toys. You should ensure that the ball is not small enough to be swallowed, and that the stick isn't a light one which can damage the structures at the back of the throat. All the time dogs are playing they are using energy, and working at the direction of the boss dog. Some working dogs will even go to sleep with a tennis ball lying next to their mouth, so that they are ready for action the instant they wake up.

Boredom

DOES YOUR DOG HAVE ENOUGH SPACE?
A bored dog is not a happy dog. The Petcare Information and Advisory Service first produced a report in 1993, 'Pets in Urban Areas', later updated by Harlock Jackson in a 2010 report 'Four Legs Four Walks', which looked

at the implications for dogs who live in apartments and housing estates. Often it means there is less space and less back yard — if, indeed, there is any at all — in which the dog can exercise and play. The report, prepared by the Melbourne animal behaviourist Dr Robert Holmes, together with the planning and development consultants Harlock Jackson and architects Goad Fink, encouraged builders and developers to design pet-friendly houses and estates. This included giving the animals access to sun and shade, outside spaces in which to exercise and plenty of windows from which to view the outside world. If a dog spends its days outside in the yard, it should be contained by a fence which allows the stimulation of a view through to the street. A bored dog which is left locked in a yard enclosed by a high paling fence is more likely to be driven to dig up the garden or pull down the washing. It is the canine equivalent of solitary confinement for human beings. The report concluded:

> On the whole a dog's behaviour is likely to be better if he or she can see a busy scene such as a busy street. Restraining a dog to a service yard with no view for long periods increases the chance of boredom which may result in undesirable behaviour such as excessive barking. Although the dog may bark at passers-by in the street, there will be less likelihood of excessive barking that might arise through boredom. It should be added that in a very busy street, a dog's tendency to bark at passers-by is likely to be considerably reduced because of the intensity of the stimulation.

It is important for owners living in high density situations to choose their breed accordingly. The report recommends small dogs such as Cavalier King Charles Spaniels or miniature Poodles for people living in units or apartments; Welsh Corgis or West Highland White Terriers for owners living in multi-dwelling developments such as villa units or townhouses; and Whippets or Cocker Spaniels for people living in houses on small blocks.

COMBATING BOREDOM — DR HOLMES' FIVE-POINT PROGRAMME

Dr Holmes suggests a five-point programme to combat boredom in dogs in a paper titled 'Environment Enrichment' published in 2001. He wrote:

> Boredom is the scourge of the suburban dog. Typically the pet dog doesn't work, is not allowed to roam and spends long periods by itself. In the wild it would always have companions, have to hunt for its food, and would roam around monitoring and marking its surroundings. In domestic life there is just not enough to do and so the dog adapts in the best way it can. The ways it does so vary with temperament and opportunities for action. Such dogs are likely to be B.A.D. — to bark, be aggressive or destructive.

He stresses that young dogs, aged from three months to three years, have a much greater need for stimulus and activity than mature dogs. The five points of the programme are obedience work, free-running exercise outside the property, play, a view of the world and a chewing object.

ᗡ 1. Obedience
Obedience work has three benefits:

> Firstly, it quietens dogs down by giving them work therapy or something to replace what they would get as working dogs. Secondly, it brings dogs under better control. The commands can be used in other situations, such as telling the dog to drop if it starts to be aggressive. Thirdly, it reinforces the handler's status as leader of the dog's pack. Every act of obedience by the dog acknowledges the handler's authority ...A key point in training is to ensure that the dog responds every time a command is given. Every time the handler repeats the command he or she reduces their authority. No commands should be given when the dog cannot be made to obey. It should not be in a position of choosing whether or not to obey. The handler has to be in a position to back up her or his authority. Consistent assertiveness on the handler's part and consistent obedience on the dog's part are the basis to solving many problems.

ᗡ 2. Free-running exercise
Providing free-running (off-leash) exercise outside the property once, or preferably twice, per day is highly stimulating for dogs and quietens them down. This does not mean following owners who are running, cycling or driving, but:

letting them run as free as the wind to sniff other dogs' urine and faeces, race around, play and follow their noses. In other words, just to behave like dogs. This is far more stimulating than free-running in the back yard. Incidentally, big back yards can be just as boring as little back yards as most dogs have many hours per day to become familiar with all the features.

3. Play

Give dogs a range of toys to play with to entertain themselves when they are left on their own. These could include plastic ice-cream containers, a thick knotted rope hanging from a tree or something similar, or a car tyre hanging so that the middle is about the height of the dog's head. If possible have your dog visited by another dog of similar abilities, so that the two animals can play together. 'The potential benefits of this canine neighbourhood play group far outweigh the risks, which can be curtailed by intensive monitoring in the early stages.'

4. A view of the world

It is essential to give dogs a view of the world:

> Allowing dogs to lie for prolonged periods of the day on the boundary of the property where they can see a busy street has a pacifying effect on them. Where possible they usually choose to have as much contact as possible with the intense and diverse range of stimuli that come from the street activities. It is unfortunate that many dogs are banished to the back yard because they bark at passers-by. This is characteristic of dogs which are only let out the front

for short periods. The logical approach initially sounds to be radical and risky. That is to confine the dog at the front of the property for extended periods. It will bark for a few hours but will settle down when its need for stimulation is satisfied.

5. Chewing objects

Chewing objects, particularly bones, are important for a dog's general wellbeing. Chewing should be directed onto one thing, and discouraged on everything else so that dogs do not become used to chewing whatever is around.

Many factors influence an animal's internal state of boredom, and each dog has a different need for stimulation and activity.

> It attempts to adapt to deficiencies in ways which are often unacceptable to owners and neighbours. Confined animals can be expected to cause problems unless they receive sufficient stimuli and activities to replace what they would receive in the wild. Owners can humanely confine their animals provided that environmental enrichment is an integral part of management.

REGULAR WALKS

I have always found that walking the dog is the greatest antidote to boredom. Apart from the exercise and stimulation that the animals derive, walking helps the process of understanding your dog, because you are noticing things about it all the time. Dogs exhibit their territorial instinct whenever they go walking. The surrounding area where they walk is all part of their extended territory, and when they stop to urinate every few minutes, it is not because of a weak bladder, but because they are 'marking' their territory, and staking their claim to the area. After a dog has urinated and defecated, it will often scrape its back paws over the grass, to spread its odours and let the other dogs know that this is its territory. The dog is stating, 'I have been here before.' When dogs stop on their walk to sniff trees and lamp posts they are exploring for the scent of other animals, and they then over-mark the spot to leave their own body odour, and stake their claim to the territory.

When you say 'walkies', dogs know from your tone of voice what it means, and associate it with what has happened in the past. When you walk, take different routes, up every street and side street, so that your dog gets to know all of the area. Then, if the dog ever escapes, or gets lost, it will know how to return home. By the time the dog has familiarised itself with the area, it will know where every animal in the neighbourhood lives.

Depending on the breed, dogs should be walked four to five kilometres a day, although the need for exercise reduces as they get older. A dog has reached middle age by the time it is six, and it will need less exercise. You don't have to do the four kilometres in one go; get up in the morning and give them a two kilometres burst before you go to work, and then you can walk them again before or after dinner. It's doing you both good, and the additional benefit is that you're interacting. Being boss dog and setting the rules has to be continually reinforced by constant interaction and, while I don't expect you to go down the road yelling and screaming, you should be interacting all the time.

The Petcare Information and Advisory Service's report 'National People and Pets', published in 2006, recorded that 30 per cent of home owners said they were bothered by persistently barking dogs in their neighbourhood and that complaints regarding barking were the number one animal issue reported to councils. A clue to the reason for that anti-social behaviour is the time that dogs were found to spend on their own, without the company of family members or other animals. The survey showed 35 per cent of owners said their dog was left on its own for up to 20 hours a week, while 15 per cent said the dog was alone for between 20 and 40 hours a week. About 5 per cent said the dog spent more than 40 hours a week without company.

Those figures explain why I received so many calls on my ABC radio programme about dogs barking, or being destructive, or a nuisance. The animals are bored. If the dog is to be by itself, it should be with another dog so it can behave like a dog. Only 15 per cent of owners in the survey admitted that their dog showed destructive behaviour either frequently or occasionally when left alone, but that low figure is explained by the fact that the owner isn't home to hear the howling or barking of the distressed dog. The only way the owner could know that the dog was barking would be if a neighbour complained, but many neighbours are reluctant to jeopardise friendly relations unless the situation becomes impossible. A lot of people are putting up with the nuisance.

All dogs need free exercise, when they are allowed

off the lead, and there has to be a compromise between the dog owner and those who control the municipalities. There should be free exercise areas in all municipalities, but in many cases the attitude of the authorities is to deny dogs any free areas, which I believe is ridiculous.

You find that after a routine of walking, games, or chewing a bone, a dog goes into its own routine of snoozing. But it's only a catnap; dogs keep a weather eye on what is happening. Dogs do a lot of sleeping and waiting, but that's because they're with the boss dog. They lie around waiting for leadership.

If you're away at work all day and you haven't made arrangements for your dog to be walked while you're away, you should interact with the dog when you get home. This raises a sense of anticipation in the dog that the boss dog will leave, but he or she will also return. Interaction between dog and owner should occur at least twice a day, and if this doesn't happen, problems will surface. The obvious sign that something is wrong is that the dog is not pleased to see you. Without constant interaction with the boss dog, it becomes a leaderless dog in the back yard, rather like a child who never sees its father because he leaves for work early and comes home late. All the dogs you see in the RSPCA kennels are leaderless, and they look imploringly at the people who come to see them, as if to say, 'Will you be my boss dog?'

Dogs are social animals

One of the first things that struck me when I moved to the practice at Balwyn was the strength of the bonding between owners and their animals. I was exposed in real life to the textbook phenomenon of anthropomorphism, where owners attribute human emotions and feelings to animals. It frequently takes the form of people saying that certain treatments are cruel. But it doesn't help the dog if owners, projecting their own feelings, say the animal wouldn't like a particular treatment, or it can't go into hospital because it would fret to death. If you're dealing with a dog that is a child substitute, the anthropomorphic element can be extreme.

Anthropomorphism prevents many people from treating a dog as a dog. Dogs need to be allowed to be dogs, and they shouldn't be treated like children. They should be given time to do the things that dogs do, like sniffing, cocking their legs, and watching other dogs. If a dog doesn't socialise with other dogs, it can become very confused. When a dog comes into a house as an eight-week-old puppy, it's not going to have much chance to associate with other dogs, particularly when many people won't allow their dogs to be with other dogs. When this happens, dogs will start to treat other dogs as the enemy.

Dogs are social animals. They belong in a pack, and they must have company, and time off when we are not controlling their lives, in the same way that members of a human family need some time off to do their own thing. Dogs have learned to accept humans as surrogate members of a dog pack, but humans still don't understand the dog as well as its fellow canines do. If you own a single dog, you run the risk of it not having the time or opportunity to behave like a proper dog. It is also totally at the mercy of the human boss dog for all its interrelationships.

TWO'S COMPANY

Dogs are happiest living in pairs, and everyone who buys a second dog notices a big difference in the behaviour of their original dog, which becomes more stimulated and contented. Having a second dog also gives the owner a greater understanding of dog behaviour, by comparing and contrasting, and learning more about dogs' hierarchical social order. It's not advisable to have three dogs: just as with children, one is always left out because three's a crowd.

If you're buying a second dog, it is always advisable to get one of the opposite sex. If you get two dogs of the same sex, and they have dominant personalities, both will want to be number two in the pecking order, behind the boss dog. The only way they will sort this out will be to fight, and the fighting between two dominant dogs, or two dominant bitches, can be horrific. There are always exceptions, of course, but at eight weeks of age, when you buy a puppy, there's no way of knowing whether it will get on with a companion dog of the same sex.

The mating season

It is a myth that bitches are happier if they have one litter of puppies before they are desexed. That's a good example of anthropomorphism. Maternalism only occurs when a bitch is lactating, and the desire to reproduce only occurs when the bitch is at the peak of a season — or 'on heat'. If she's not in season, she has absolutely no interest in reproduction.

The smaller the breed, the more likely it is for the bitch to have her first season at or around six months, whereas a bigger dog is likely to have its first season between 12 and 18 months. Once the first season is over, subsequent seasons occur regularly, at intervals of about six months. There is no menopause in dogs, and they can go on reproducing until they die, although the season becomes increasingly erratic after they reach nine or 10.

The season is divided into two parts: the pro-oestrus stage, followed by the oestrus stage. During the pro-oestrus stage, which lasts about seven days, the bitch discharges an odour, and a watery blood discharge, which proclaims to male dogs that she is coming into season, and is available to be mated. In the wild, she attracts a large number of suitors, and she chooses one or more. The domesticated bitch who is being used for breeding is more likely to be presented with one male.

Once the bleeding has stopped — usually seven to 12 days after the start of the discharge — the bitch enters the true oestrus stage, when she is about to ovulate. Provided mating coincides with ovulation, pregnancy normally follows. Ovulation will occur at the time of accepting the male dog or within a maximum of three days, and during the remainder of the stage, which takes a further week, the genitalia will return to its normal resting state, and the bitch will no longer be attractive to male dogs. The whole season usually takes about 21 days.

Male dogs are inherently programmed to find bitches in season, and the only time a male dog is aroused is when he finds a bitch on heat. Many male dogs enjoy the experience, and remember it, and roam to find another bitch in season. We have domesticated most of the natural instincts of dogs, but reproduction is not one of them, so the influence of the male hormone in dogs which have not been desexed is exactly the same as you would get in dogs in the wild. Desexing will stop the production of these hormones, and the roaming of dogs looking for a mate.

Once a male dog is desexed, the male hormone level drops, and erections will cease to occur. It will no longer have any interest in bitches beyond normal dog-to-dog interaction. Dogs who are desexed will still recognise when a bitch is in season, but they won't do anything about it.

BREEDING

People often wonder whether they should breed their bitch. As a general rule, unless you're going into it commercially, with multiple breeding bitches, you will not make any money. The dog has become so domesticated that human intervention is usually necessary to ensure success in the breeding process, and in rearing the puppies. The amount of intervention depends very much on the individual bitch, and whether she has a lot of problems. If she is a terrific mother the process generally goes without a hitch. Each puppy born into a litter is an individual, just as each child is, and the more puppies a bitch has, the more problems you are likely to have. Even if you have a very beautiful dog or bitch, with a great temperament, the characteristics will not necessarily be passed on to the progeny.

As soon as the bitch's milk dries up, which usually happens after six to eight weeks, she loses the maternal streak and starts preparing for her next litter. She has to toss these puppies out and get on with life. They are converted from her puppies to young dog associates.

You also have to consider the difficulties associated with disposing of the puppies. If they're pure breeds, homes will probably be found comparatively easily, but finding homes for cross breeds is much harder. For all these reasons, most owners decide breeding is too hard, and have their animals desexed — a view fully encouraged by the RSPCA.

Correct feeding and sleeping habits

Over-feeding is not the way to make your dog happy. There are recommended weights for pure breeds, and you should stick to them. If you brush your fingertips over the rib cage of your dog, you should just be able to feel its ribs. If you can't, you're giving it too much to eat. Labradors and Golden Retrievers are two examples of breeds that are quick to put on weight if they are over-fed and under-exercised. Owners don't consider that the big dog which lies down and does nothing will put on weight: they don't think it through, and it never occurs to them that the reason they're fat is the same reason why the dog is fat. It's a case of one piece of cake for me, and one for the dog; one biscuit for me, and one for the dog.

If a correct feeding regime is essential to a dog's

happiness, so is having its own proper place to sleep. The reason dogs sleep in baskets is that they like to have their own personal space, just as humans do. They also have their possessions, like tennis balls and bones. Bones are precious, and a dog will growl and snarl if you try and take its bone away while it is still chewing it. Dogs bury bones to make sure that no other dog gets its teeth on them. It's like humans putting possessions away in a drawer or safe.

Dogs have an associative memory, and they remember things that are pleasurable, and things that are nasty. The memory can be triggered by a smell or a noise. Often dogs dislike going to the veterinary surgery, and they may associate the smell there with something unpleasant that happened to them, like an injection. I'm told that dogs who are treated by me will leave the room when they hear me talking on the radio, because my voice is imprinted.

If there's one thing that will get a dog moving faster than hearing my voice, it's a cat. It's often said that dogs hate cats, but they love chasing them. When a dog spots a cat across the road it sees an animal that is frightened and runs away, setting up the chase. In the stand-off the dog is usually the one that will back off, after the cat has fluffed up its fur and given a warning hiss.

A dog's mood is judged by its tail attitude, and that's why I'm so opposed to dogs having their tails cut off — or 'docked'. For instance, how does a Rottweiler with a docked tail communicate that it's happy? While the unhappy, fearful dog slinks with its tail between its legs, the happy dog will wag its tail. The happy dog is usually bright and alert, with its ears pricked up, and it often vocalises in a higher-pitched yip. When a dog rolls over on its back, asking to be scratched on the stomach, it's a sign of submission and absolute willingness to do the bidding of the boss dog.

The happy dog has learned that life is predictable: it has proper guidance, established routines, and set times to interact with the boss dog. A well-adjusted dog with a good rapport with the boss dog will always be contented, because there is a certainty to life.

The happy dog also has an owner who ensures that the animal is properly housed, fed and exercised, and that it receives the right parasite control. If all this is done, the animal's welfare is guaranteed, and you won't need to visit the vet.

CONTENTED OWNERS

Dogs continue to maintain their popularity. The 2010 nationwide survey for the Australian Companion Animal Council (ACAC) found that 36 per cent of Australian households had a dog compared with 23 per cent in the United Kingdom and 40 per cent in the United States. The total number of dogs in Australia at 3.41 million makes Australians the highest per capita owners of dogs in the world.

The survey confirms what vets constantly witness in practice, namely that the dog is winning the popularity contest with the cat, because of its dependability and high level of interaction with humans. 'Dogs won't let you down' is the common cry of owners frustrated with the human race. Dogs like doing things with humans, and will provide emotional support, while at the same time being willing to be dominated and directed by humans. They appear to understand human moods and seem able to overcome the communication barrier, even though they can't speak.

You can never be quite sure that you own a cat (I actually have two). The cat associates with you, rather than necessarily wanting you warts 'n' all. It stands aloof, and usually only wants to interact with you on its own terms. It's the emotional reverse of the dog, which is highly dependent on humans.

The support role played by dogs was reflected in the fact that 79 per cent of owners in the survey said they found it comforting to be with their pet 'when things go wrong'. And 91 per cent said they felt 'very close' to their pet, indicating that it was seen as an integral part of the family.

The PIAS National People and Pets survey in 2006 confirmed how strongly embedded the dog is in the family unit. The highest dog ownership rate — 49 per cent — occurred in married couples with dependents, followed by lone parents with dependents at 41 per cent. The lowest dog ownership rates were among lone people aged less than 35 (18.9 per cent), and lone people over 60 (15.8 per cent).

The survey also indicated the extent to which pet ownership becomes a habit: 82 per cent of households had previously owned a cat or dog, and 74 per cent of households who did not currently have pets had previously kept a cat or a dog; while 12 per cent of households with cats or dogs had never kept them before.

The most common reason for not owning cats or dogs was that they were too much bother (22 per cent), the lease prohibited it (19 per cent), or because it restricted other activities (15 per cent).

Studies also show that the dog is a great social facilitator, and will break the ice between people who might not otherwise speak to each other. Respondents in the National People and Pets survey said, 'I make better social contacts through having a dog', a statement that would be supported by most veterinarians who find that conversation is quickly struck up in their waiting rooms by owners exchanging notes on breeds and behaviour. It is the opposite of the stoney silence that you find in most doctors' waiting rooms.

I meet lots of owners for whom the dog is number two in the family, and wives, husbands and children come after the dog. I'm continually amazed at the way people attach themselves to the most smelly, indescribably badly-behaved dogs. In some cases these owners have had relationships with humans, but they've failed, and the dog has remained constant throughout. Some people have commented that the growth of dog ownership has coincided with the breakdown of the extended family, and certainly you see that young people who break away from home often have a dog, perhaps for constancy in a sea of change.

In the National People and Pets survey 17 out of 20 dog owners gave companionship as the main function of their pet, and one-third gave protection as a secondary function. Plenty of people had tried cats as companion animals when they moved into units, as the body corporate regulations forbade dogs, but the experiment generally failed because cats were unable to produce the level of interaction wanted by the owner. Many people ignore the regulations and acquire small dogs, which are never seen during the day. The importance of the bond between animals and elderly people, particularly single ones, has been recognised by some retirement villages that have pet zones, enabling people to continue dog ownership.

Dog ownership is good for your health

Earlier studies had found that people's blood pressure dropped when stroking animals, or from simply being in the presence of animals. The ACAC 2010 report confirms that dog owners benefited both physically and mentally from having an animal. Dog owners are physically more active than non-pet owners and report greater satisfaction with their physical fitness. They visit the doctor less often, and are less likely to take medication for high blood pressure, sleeping difficulties, high cholesterol or heart problems.

The health benefits of dog companionship were found to be greatest among those people who would be most likely to visit the doctor, such as older men and women. People living on their own, such as divorcees or widows, were also shown to derive special benefit from dog ownership. It's very easy to be alone and lonely, and clients have frequently told me that having the dog to talk to when they get home has saved their sanity. With family units becoming smaller, the dog becomes more important because we've made them fill the emotional gaps in our lives.

The first worldwide study on the links between improved health and pet ownership was conducted in the early 1980s by American researcher Erica Friedmann, who was investigating whether a person's social life and their degree of social isolation might influence their ability to survive a heart attack. She conducted extensive interviews with 92 convalescing male patients, and after 14 of the men had died within a year, she tried to discover the differentiating features between those who had survived and those who died.

Friedmann found that socially isolated people were more likely to succumb to heart disease, and that those with pets were more likely to recover. She concluded that there was a slight fall in the probability of death among pet owners recovering from heart disease. I can support the conclusions of this study from my own experience in practice, as I see many clients who say their recovery from heart disease was helped by going for walks with their dog.

In 1991 an English research team under James Serpell found that the acquisition of a pet was associated with a reduced incidence of minor health problems and an improvement in psychological wellbeing. A year later Professor Warwick Anderson, Deputy Director of the Baker Medical Research Institute in Melbourne, led a team which reported that pet owners had significantly lower risk factors for cardiovascular disease, including lower blood pressure. One reason may have been that pet owners took significantly more exercise than non-owners.

In 1992 the Petcare Information and Advisory Service commissioned a report 'What Australians Feel About Their Pets', and it concluded that in this 'Age of Anxiety', people were turning to their pets for comfort to overcome their feelings of isolation, loss of control, and loss of confidence. The report also suggested that in this politically correct world, when everyone has to think twice about what they say about anything, it was an immense relief to be able to say what you liked to the dog, without fear or inhibition: 'Pet owners appreciate the fact that, in relationship to their pets, there is no pressure to act in a certain way.'

Building on the early Serpell and Anderson work there have been many further studies on the influence of pet ownership on human health. These are summarised in the PIAS National People and Pets 2006 Report titled 'Living Well Together'. More specific information is included in the following reports: 'Is dog ownership or dog walking associated with weight status in children and their parents?', 'The pet connection: pets as a conduit to social capital' and 'Does getting a dog increase recreational walking?' which can all be found on the Anthrozoology website.

The bond between people and dogs

The close bond between animal and human is at the heart of the mental and emotional benefits enjoyed by dog owners. The bond changes through all the different stages of life. Children will see a dog on equal terms and view it as a friend, and also as a buffer zone against adults. Young adults no longer treat the dog as an equal, but it becomes enormously important as a companion: it's often a case of 'me and the dog versus the world'.

For young married couples the dog is a shared bond, and it can reach high levels of intensity if the animal takes on the role of a child substitute. In couples with children, the dog becomes an essential ingredient of the family unit. As the children grow up, the family dog is often seen by the husband as his personal mate. Where the mother stays at home, an equally intense relationship may develop, and the unit becomes 'Mum, the kids, and the dog'.

When the children leave home, and particularly after the death of a spouse, the remaining partner often turns to the dog for companionship, and it becomes the only remaining link between the surviving person and the marriage. Euthanasia is always traumatic, but it is most distressing when I'm asked to put down a dog that was the last link with a marriage partner, or if the dog is the only animal a child has ever known.

Malcolm McHarg, the manager of the People and Pets survey, had conducted previous research in 1976. He concluded from the new study that dog owners had become more responsible in the intervening 20 years, particularly over the issues of getting dogs vaccinated, exercising them, and picking up their dog's faeces. The 1995 survey found that most owners kept their animals on a lead during exercise, and troublesome barking or destructive behaviour by the dog was relatively uncommon.

It reported that the great majority of pet owners were responsible and considerate carers. While this kind of owner certainly exists, I have frequently encountered arrogant dog owners who are only interested in themselves and their dogs. I have found in life that there are three pointers to human behaviour: one is the way people ride their bike, another is the way they drive their car, and the third is the way they own dogs. Owners often take the attitude that it's their dog, and it's their business what they do with it. They show little consideration for humans or other dogs.

Most of the difficulties experienced with uncontrolled dogs are due to irresponsible owners. This has led to a growing belief among those involved with animal welfare that owners should be licensed by local councils as fit and proper people to own a dog.

Off-leash exercise

Consideration will be required from all sides to resolve two of the most controversial dog ownership issues currently facing local municipalities in Australia. The first is the exercise of dogs in public parks, and the second is defecation by dogs in public areas. There is growing conflict between dog owners and the anti-dog lobby over whether animals should be allowed free running areas in public parks. Attempts by municipalities to impose regulations that dogs should always be kept on a leash have provoked a strong reaction from dog owners, who are often the highest users of the parks.

The municipalities of Boroondara, in Melbourne, and Rockingham, outside Perth, have both experienced a fierce backlash from dog owners suddenly threatened with having to walk their dogs on a leash at all times. There was a similar reaction in Santa Monica, in California, when dogs were banned from public parks. The dog lobby exerted pressure on the local authorities and dogs were eventually provided with two parks where they were allowed off the leash in the early morning and late afternoon.

PART 2 BEHAVIOUR

RSPCA policy states that dogs should be kept on a leash in public places, but it also recommends that where such a requirement exists, the local municipality must provide a series of spaces where dogs are permitted to exercise off-leash. These spaces should be signposted to advise anyone entering them that they may meet with unleashed dogs.

In the People and Pets survey 60 per cent of owners said they always kept their dog on a leash when exercising in public places, which suggests to me that some respondents were giving the politically correct reply rather than the true answer. I think it would be closer to the mark to say that 80 per cent of owners had a dog lead on their person, but not necessarily on the dog. The most contentious dog ownership issue has been animals not being kept on leads, and if 60 per cent of owners kept their dog on a lead, as the survey states, we would not have had so much community unrest stemming from dog bite incidents which are virtually reported daily.

The survey stated 50 per cent of owners said they walked their dog once or twice a day; 26 per cent said they walked it most days, but not every day; and 20 per cent said they walked their dog once or twice a week. Only 2 per cent admitted to walking the animal less than once a week. One of the most common causes of complaint to the RSPCA from members of the public is that they see neighbours' dogs which are never let off a chain. In many cases there is no doubt that unless the dog is being walked at 2 am, it is getting no exercise at all.

The survey reported that women were twice as likely to walk the dog than men, which does not surprise me. It is in the nature of women to be more planned and consistent, and in child-rearing they are more often the ones who see that things happen, and that the children go to the doctor and the dentist. There is no doubt the male gets a great deal out of the relationship with a dog, but it's often a one-way relationship. That doesn't mean men don't have a great attachment to the dog, but they allocate their time elsewhere, and it's usually the woman who brings the dog for its vaccination or takes it for its daily walk. The only finding in the survey that confirmed the male's much-vaunted special relationship with dogs was that where dogs were exercised several times a day, it was more likely that a man would be the walker.

The most common places for exercise and walking were local streets (54 per cent), and parks or other public places, excluding beaches and the banks of rivers or creeks (48 per cent). Dogs get far more interest and excitement by having their walks varied, because they have a wonderful sense of smell, which is stimulated by venturing into new territory. Going through busy, familiar places can also appeal to dogs, because other dogs may have marked the territory since the last walk, and other things may have happened.

Dog control laws are necessary for the safety and wellbeing of dogs, as well as humans. But dog owners will only support the laws if they see that municipalities adopt a balanced approach, taking into account the needs of dog owners and non-dog owners. Each time a privilege like freedom for dogs in all public places is removed it must be replaced with a new privilege, namely freedom for dogs in designated areas.

Dogs need exercise for exactly the same reasons humans do, namely to keep fit and healthy, and this can be achieved on the leash, provided the owner ensures the dog covers adequate distance, and varies the pace of the exercise. Off-leash exercise ensures the dog will cover the required distance, and establish its own pace. If dogs don't get the right sort of exercise, they will end up like 80 per cent of the dogs who come to my surgery, unfit and overweight.

The issue of exercise for dogs in public spaces will become increasingly important for local municipalities, and it is important that they develop constructive policies which take into account the needs of both sides. The Petcare Information and Advisory Service published a report titled 'Public Open Space and Dogs' which gives local municipalities strategic guidelines on how to develop free running areas for dogs within public parks. Written by Virginia Jackson, an urban planner, with the assistance of Professor Judith Blackshaw, from the veterinary science department of the University of Queensland, and Jane Marriott, a landscape designer, it gives detailed suggestions about how these free exercise spaces should be planned, so that they avoid children's playgrounds and other sensitive areas.

The report attempts to move away from the 'us and them' conflict over dogs which has recently split municipalities like Boroondara and Rockingham, and instead of presenting dog owners as a problem (which is how they tend to have been seen in the past), they are seen as a legitimate and sizable community group. The benefit for the community is that if dogs are allowed free running areas where they can use up their energy, they are less likely to become bored at home, and therefore less likely to bark and indulge in other anti-social behaviour.

PICK UP THE POO
Defecation by dogs is closely linked to the issue of off-leash exercise, and is the reason why so many ratepayers oppose dogs in public parks. Australia has lagged behind other countries such as England, France, and the US, which have introduced regulations ensuring that faeces are picked up by dog owners and, in some cases, placed in special bins provided by the local municipality. Councils on Sydney's North Shore have led the way in legislating for the removal of faeces, and the People and Pets survey found that 48 per cent of Sydney dog owners said they always picked up their dog's droppings, compared with 36 per cent in other Australian cities; 42 per cent of owners said they never picked up their dog's faeces. There are new local municipal anti-fouling laws in all urban areas of Australia.

Anti-fouling laws may at least assist in making people aware of the fact that they should be considerate to others, but if municipalities introduce regulations, they must make it easy for owners to dispose of their dog's faeces, through the provision of bins, or pooper scoopers. Who is going to pick up their dog's droppings, put it in a plastic bag, and keep it in their pocket for the rest of the walk? But if two or three bins are provided in the park, people's social consciences will be pricked.

It's a hygiene issue rather than a health or animal welfare issue, and medical people greatly exaggerate the health risk from dog faeces containing roundworm eggs. If these eggs are swallowed by humans, it can cause liver, eye, or brain problems due to dog roundworm larvae migrating through the human bowel wall and the larvae being spread to these organs via the bloodstream.

The major threat is children playing with the faecal material, or touching the dog around its rear end, and not washing their hands. The real problem is the owner not worming the dog, rather than allowing the dog to defecate in the park — however unhygienic that might appear. It should be remembered that healthy dogs can also catch whipworm, hookworm and parvovirus by sniffing or licking the area where infected dogs have defecated.

Should people replace deceased dogs?

The People and Pets survey confirmed that pet ownership tends to be a lifetime habit, begun in childhood and continued through the various stages of life. Often the only reason people break the habit is because they move house, and there is insufficient space for the dog to exercise. Of those currently owning a dog, 76 per cent intend replacing it when it dies. The other 24 per cent give the following two reasons for non-replacement: 'I expect to be too upset' or 'I do not want the responsibility'.

I have found that a third reason for non-replacement is that old people fear that if they buy a new dog they will die before the dog, leaving it homeless. But often the owners live much longer than they think, and they spend years of unnecessary misery, when they could be sharing their life with a pet. They should also remember that, in many cases, five years is half a dog's life. In my long experience I have rarely put down a dog because 'no-one would take it'. Owners also have the added reassurance of knowing that they may join the RSPCA's bequest foster programme, which provides them with the certainty that their dog will be given a home should it outlast the owner.

The two great truths of dog ownership are that, if you do it properly, the care of the dog will be a constant, ongoing responsibility. You will also form a close emotional attachment, which may be very painful to sever. I have often found that it's only when I come to put a dog down, and see the distress it causes the owner, that the full extent of the bond between the two becomes clear.

The temporary distress of losing the dog is far outweighed by the rewards of ownership: you will be fitter and happier, and you'll have a friend for life.

3

Health

GETTING RID OF THE PESTS

As a young veterinary student in Brisbane, I remember being told by John Sprent, Professor of Veterinary Parasitology, that more harm was done to animals by parasites than any other factor. I was startled by this statement at the time, thinking viruses and bacteria probably did more damage, but the 45 years that I have spent in practice have confirmed that parasites have a profound influence on the health of animals. Perhaps the veterinary profession hasn't emphasised this enough in the past in the case of companion animals. Production animals like sheep and dairy cattle have always received plenty of attention because parasite infections reduce the output of the animals, but there was never quite the same economic imperative in getting the message across for dogs and cats kept as household pets.

It's only when you come into contact with affected animals that you realise how vicious parasites can be, and when vets advise people to worm their animals routinely, and maintain a good flea control programme, they aren't simply looking to make another sale of flea rinses or worm tablets. As three of the parasites — puppy roundworm, sarcoptic mange and hydatid tapeworm — can also affect humans, it becomes doubly important for them to be controlled.

Dogs are highly dependent on their human owners, and never more so than in the ongoing battle with the pests which can make a misery of a dog's life, and at worst, even threaten its life. Fleas, mites, ticks and lice cause irritation to the skin, while worms irritate the lining of the bowel, often leading to diarrhoea and, in extreme cases, vomiting. These conditions can be highly aggravating to a dog, and owners must be constantly vigilant to prevent and, if necessary, treat an infestation.

Ear mites

Ear mites are small, wingless insects which are so tiny that they can only be detected by using an auriscope with a magnifying eyepiece. They irritate the dog by chewing at the lining of the ear canal, and the body tries to compensate by producing excessive ear wax, which is usually the first sign of mites. Another is that a dog will scratch its ears with its hind legs, or even sit with its head cocked to one side.

Like fleas, ear mites are soil insects. They are frequently picked up in the first few weeks after birth, though the clinical symptoms may not appear until several weeks later. Treatment is by insecticidal ear drops, which quickly kill the adults, but it's essential that you also kill the new mites, which hatch from eggs laid in the hairs around the entrance to the ear. Use insecticidal 'spot-on' drops. Check any other cats and dogs in the house because ear mites are highly contagious. I would recommend using spot-on drops on all animals in the household where ear mites have been diagnosed.

Fleas

The first thing to be understood about fleas is that they are a soil insect which reproduces in dry dirt containing plenty of humus. They jump onto a dog when it lies down in dirt, and once they are carried in the dog's coat, they will transfer onto carpet or bedding. They will also jump from dog to dog, and from cat to dog. They do not live on dogs, and the only reason they bother attaching themselves to dogs is to reproduce. They need to suck fresh dog's blood, which contains substances that trigger the laying of an average of 1500 eggs per flea.

Fleas enjoy warmth and dryness, so they are less of a problem outdoors in winter, particularly in the southern states, but the growing problem we face is that central heating in our houses creates the perfect climate for the hatching of flea eggs throughout the year. Certainly, vets are now tending to see flea-allergic dermatitis all year round, whereas the traditional season used to be from October till the end of autumn.

Treatment involves killing the fleas on the dog, as well as the fleas in their environment; be they in bedding, in the carpet or, in a dry dirt patch, for example, under the house. It is no good killing the fleas if the animal is immediately re-infested when it returns to its basket or its favourite place in the back yard. Fleas can be killed by using specific spot-on insecticidal drops. Dogs can be prevented from lying in the dirt by fencing off the most troublesome areas. Dogs' bedding should be washed weekly at the height of the flea season, and that should include an insecticide rinse.

Insecticides and growth retardants in aerosol cans may be used to kill fleas and eggs in domestic carpets. Each 125g container does about two standard-sized rooms, so four cans are usually needed for the average suburban house. Each treatment lasts from three to six months.

There is a range of products which are effective in killing fleas. The decision whether to choose a powder, a rinse or an internal insecticide largely depends on how effectively and consistently you have to apply the product. Many dogs are hard to handle when applying external insecticides because they object to the odour.

By far the best treatment is to use spot-on products which come in the form of a liquid that is applied every four weeks to the skin at the base of the dog's neck, between the shoulder blades. The insecticide is absorbed into the skin fat, and when the flea bites into the skin it absorbs the insecticide and dies.

Flea powders last for three days, and most flea rinses work for five days, although they are immediately rendered useless if the dog goes swimming in a creek or runs under the garden sprinkler, and the insecticide is washed off the coat.

Another form of flea treatment is to use growth inhibitor tablets, which prevent flea eggs from becoming fertile. The fleas still bite the dog, but they don't lay fertile eggs and over time there are less adult fleas to irritate dogs. The tablets need to be taken for at least six months before they begin to decrease the actual flea eggs in a dog's environment. Dogs who go on these tablets can expect a much easier time in summer, when fleas are at their worst.

With all these products, you must use and re-use them, according to the directions, and not when the mood suits you.

It has been estimated that in human medicine only 70 per cent of patients comply with treatment regimes set by their doctors. The compliance rate would be much less in veterinary medicine, where you have the additional problems of dogs refusing to swallow a tablet or to be bathed. Vets have an ironic saying, 'When all else fails, read the directions', and that pretty well sums up the attitude of some clients. It's instructive to recall that most dogs poisoned by snail bait are poisoned in their own homes, even though the directions on the snail bait packet clearly spell out the dangers. Many people simply don't read or absorb the instructions, and are highly critical when their dog doesn't get better. Many dog owners are looking for a magic button to get rid of a problem, and that doesn't exist.

Lice

Lice are the least common of the pests, and I have only seen two cases of infested dogs in 45 years. They are larger than fleas and live their entire life cycle on the dog, scuttling along the surface of the skin, and laying their eggs at the base of the hairs. Affected dogs are unkempt, usually haven't been groomed or washed for years, and look thoroughly unhygienic. The treatment is insecticidal spot-on drops which must be repeated regularly until all signs of lice eggs laid at the base of the coat hairs disappears.

Mange

The description 'mangey' stems from the mange caused by the sarcoptes mite, which is caught by dogs that have been in contact with mange-infected wildlife, like fox or wombat carcases. The condition is frequently seen in dogs that live in the outer suburbs, or go to the bush for weekends. It can also be contracted by humans, usually where their skin has brushed against the affected part of the dog's coat, and often results in a rash on the forearm or in the webs of the fingers.

The most commonly affected areas of a dog are around the head, and the edges of the ear flaps, which become thickened and scaly. A dog suffering from mange will be far more irritated than it would be with a heavy flea infestation, and usually it can't stop scratching. Treatment consists of several internal injections of an insecticide by a vet, together with an insecticidal bath which will produce a dramatic lowering of the irritation and the scratching. Continue the treatment until the coat hair is growing again.

Demodex mange

The demodex mange mite does not possess a tough cuticle coat, so to survive it burrows into the hair follicles of the dog's skin, breaking the hair off, and making it appear as though the dog is going bald. Every puppy acquires demodectic mites from its mother, but most never exhibit clinical symptoms because of the defence provided by the immune system. It's only if the puppy has a poor immune system that it will contract the condition. Bull Terriers and the German breeds, like the German Shepherd and Dachshund, are more susceptible to the disease.

Small, bare patches appear on the head or the feet, and after some time these patches develop pustules which result in the skin becoming very irritated, causing the dog to scratch or chew the areas. The demodectic mange then spreads slowly to other parts of the body. It is not transmissible to humans. Treatment is difficult, because it is hard to get the required insecticide to penetrate the hair follicle, where the mite is living. A special rinse has been developed, but a more effective treatment is to have your vet give the affected dog a series of injections of internal insecticide.

Ticks

Ticks are wingless, blood-sucking insects which are most common in the warmer areas of Australia. They can occur as far south as Lakes Entrance in Victoria, but it is unusual to find them in southern Victoria or Tasmania, unless an owner has recently returned from a trip to northern Australia with the dog. Like fleas, they are most common in the warm spring and summer months.

The adult tick lives in the soil, and dogs pick up tick larvae when they brush through grass. The larvae, or tick nymphs as they are called, attach themselves to dogs, and start sucking their blood, which enables them to transform into an adult tick. These ticks usually attach themselves to the skin folds, particularly in the head and neck area, and are also often found around the ears, lips and eyelids. They become bloated to the size of a large pea after sucking blood for five to seven days. The difference between fleas and ticks is that the tick buries its biting parts into the skin to suck blood, and so it's immobile, whereas the flea jumps around.

One species of tick, *Ixodes holocyclus*, can cause paralysis and even death in a dog. To help them suck blood, all ticks pump anti-coagulant saliva into the dog's skin, but the saliva of *Ixodes holocyclus* is toxic to the dog's nervous system. The risk of serious illness to the dog makes it terribly important for an owner to kill any tick nymphs that get onto their dog by using an acaricidal insecticidal rinse or use a specific spot-on treatment.

Ticks have a tough cuticle coat, and a strong insecticide is needed to kill them. In tick areas, or before entering these areas, you should apply the specific spot-on insecticidal drops fortnightly during the tick season from September to March as a prophylactic. Continue treatment for a month after leaving tick areas. You should also examine the dog daily around the head and neck to look for any adult ticks which may have survived the insecticide. If you discover an adult tick, crush the head by using a pair of eyebrow tweezers.

Worms

Fleas are visible and the distress they cause to dogs is obvious. But far more sinister is the threat posed to dogs by worms. In the case of bowel worms, they rob the dog of nourishment, and create serious inflammatory reactions in the dog's bowel, while heartworm poses a danger to the dog's life by destroying the valves and lining of the heart. Fleas get more attention, but the internal parasites that are unseen can more commonly lead to death.

Even today, after so many years in practice, I'm continually amazed when I receive the results of clinical pathology tests performed on sick dogs, and discover that the primary reason for the illness is a heavy worm burden in the bowel. It happens because the owners don't practise preventative medicine by worming their dogs, and it's only when the worms become established in the bowel that they notice signs that the dog is not well. Just as you vaccinate your dog annually, so should you regularly give it tablets to prevent worms.

Dogs can be infested by four different bowel worms: roundworm, hookworm, whipworm and tapeworm. The life cycle of all except the tapeworm involves the production of eggs by adult worms in the bowel, which are passed by the dog in its droppings, and these in turn re-infect the dog, or other dogs, when they pick the eggs up off the ground and swallow them.

ROUNDWORM

Roundworms look like a creamy-brown garden worm, and normally live in the first part of the bowel after the stomach. They lie together, partially blocking the bowel, and this causes bowel irritation and in heavy infestations, vomiting and diarrhoea.

Roundworm treatment is essential for all puppies because they are infected by their mothers before birth. It is important that pregnant bitches are wormed, because puppies can be born with quite a heavy infestation of roundworm. In serious cases puppies will sometimes vomit up roundworm. The first dose should be given between two and a half and three weeks of age, and repeated fortnightly until three months. From three to 12 months the dog should be treated monthly, and from then on, every three months for the rest of the dog's life. Roundworm eggs can cause serious illness if swallowed by humans. The eggs cause the release in the bowel of larvae, which penetrate the bowel wall, and enter the bloodstream, resulting in very serious reactions in the human liver, brain, or eye.

HOOKWORM
Hookworm is a blood-sucking parasite which occurs in the small bowel and rapidly causes anaemia and weight loss. It thrives in mud and very wet conditions, and the larvae can penetrate the skin of a dog's feet. Hookworm can be treated with special tablets, but nowadays most broad spectrum worming tablets will treat roundworm, hookworm and whipworm in the one dose.

WHIPWORM
Whipworm lives in the caecum (the junction between the small and large bowel), and as its name suggests, it looks like a long, single-threaded whip. It causes great irritation in the lower bowel, resulting in uncontrollable diarrhoea, haemorrhaging from the bowel and loss of bodyweight. Whipworm eggs can live in the soil for up to 10 years after they've been passed by a dog, so once an area has been contaminated, it's very difficult to eliminate

the source. Fire is very effective, but incinerating your property is an expensive way of getting rid of whipworm.

TAPEWORM

Tapeworm and the hydatid tapeworm both differ from the other three worms because they go through a secondary life cycle. In the case of the common tapeworm, this secondary life cycle is in the dog flea, while in the hydatid tapeworm, it is in sheep. Dogs become infested with tapeworm when they eat an infected flea, and they become infested with the hydatid tapeworm when they eat infected offal from sheep, which is either deliberately in their diet or from sheep carcases.

Tapeworm live in the small part of the bowel and cause anal irritation, which dogs show by scooting on their bottom. They are usually diagnosed by the owner who notices pinkish-white segments crawling out of the dog's anus when it is at rest or, alternatively, the worms may be sighted crawling over the surface of a bowel motion. Many general dog wormers do not treat tapeworm, so you must use a product specifically designed to combat it. An adult dog should be treated for tapeworm every three months, at the same time it is treated for other worm types. Dogs which live in or visit sheep farming areas should be wormed against hydatids every six weeks.

Hydatid tapeworm eggs swallowed by humans can cause bladder cysts to form in the chest and bowel cavities. These have serious consequences and surgical treatment is horrific.

HEARTWORM

The heartworm is potentially one of the most dangerous of all the worms. The adult heartworm lives in the right-side chamber of the heart, and can grow to 30 cm long. It causes great destruction to the heart chamber, eventually leading to right heart failure. The female heartworm releases tiny, tadpole-like larvae called microfilaria into the bloodstream, and these are picked up by mosquitoes, which inject the larvae into other dogs. Prevention of the disease is a great deal more reliable than treatment, and the tablets work by killing the larvae before they develop into heartworm. They are highly effective provided they are used regularly, as prescribed.

Puppies should begin taking daily or monthly tablets to protect them against heartworm by the time they are three months old. The monthly chewable tablet is more expensive, but it frees the owner from the task of administering a tablet daily. Some owners like giving the daily tablet because it gives them the opportunity to interact with their dog, but you should be wary that a lot of dogs get cunning, and owners suddenly look behind the sofa and find a fortnight's supply of heartworm tablets that were supposed to have been swallowed. There's no room for error with the daily tablets, and if you miss two days in a row, you're in trouble. You can be up to 10 days late with the monthly tablet without putting the dog in danger. Better still get your vet to use an annual treatment against heartworm by injection.

PART 3 HEALTH

When you purchase a dog, you may not realise that dog ownership is quite complex, and there are all sorts of accidents which can happen, and diseases it can catch. Dog ownership entails consistent responsibilities, one of which is understanding the importance of preventative medicine, and that, without our help, dogs won't survive. Humans learn survival skills as they go through life, but because dogs cannot speak for themselves, humans must learn survival skills on behalf of their dog.

A CASE FOR THE VET

The lesson that Tom Ewer, Professor of Animal Husbandry at the University of Queensland, taught me when I was his student has seemed more and more relevant to me in nearly 45 years of practice: unless you understand normal behaviour in a dog, you have no hope of understanding what is abnormal, and, more particularly, of recognising the warning signs that the dog is ill. A dog that is unwell, or that has suffered an injury, will always give clear signs that it is sick or has a problem with some part of its anatomy. Owners must spend time observing their dog and all its idiosyncrasies — how it walks, jumps, and eats its food — because a change to the dog's normal pattern of behaviour will be a pointer to what's wrong. Your dog's behavioural pattern can't be learned in a textbook, and the only way to understand it is to observe the dog and interact with it at least twice a day.

A well dog will be alert, bright-eyed, interested in what's going on, and it will look for and relish its food and drink. The cardinal signs of something wrong are depression (or hiding); unwillingness to move; and refusing food. The other key signs are vomiting for more than 12 hours; diarrhoea for longer than 24 hours; lameness or an inability to use a limb for more than

24 hours; sore or inflamed eyes; pus discharge; blood loss from any orifice; and lethargy, or wanting to sleep continuously.

Following is a brief guide to the warning signs given by different parts of the dog's body to indicate that something is wrong.

Abdominal cavity

The abdominal cavity includes the stomach and bowel, liver, pancreas, kidneys and urinary system and, in the female dog, the reproductive system. A dog with a stomach or bowel complaint will refuse to eat. If the dog vomits blood, or has blood in any diarrhoea, the cause should be investigated immediately.

Kidney disease is usually characterised by failure to eat, or a reduced desire for food and sometimes vomiting and diarrhoea. The animal will drink more, and it will lose bodyweight. Often you find increased frequency of urination, and the urine will sometimes be bloody-pink and contain clots or streaks of blood. The urinary system is the major excretory system in the body, and it does frequently become diseased.

Inflammation of the bladder, or cystitis, makes a relatively healthy dog urinate more often, but with small amounts of urine that is often blood-coloured. Most cystitis in dogs occurs as a result of stones in the bladder.

Older female dogs often wet their bed, or the area where they're lying, during sleep. This is caused by a hormonal imbalance, which can be treated by hormone replacement therapy.

The liver is such an important organ that when liver disease strikes, it happens very rapidly, and the animal quickly becomes very ill. The dog will go off its food completely, is often in a state of collapse and usually vomiting. In very serious cases, the surrounds of the eyes and the lining of the mouth show the classic yellow colour of jaundice.

One of the most under-diagnosed or mis-diagnosed infections in dogs is pancreatitis. It can range from a minor inflammation, where a dog will simply go off its food, to serious inflammation, where it can be hunched up in acute pain, with vomiting and diarrhoea. Disease of the pancreas, like the liver, can be critical, and dogs that are seriously ill with pancreatitis should be treated as a medical emergency.

Brain

The most usual signs of brain disease are fitting, followed by a short period of disorientation. These fits can range from being quite mild, up to the most serious seizures. Other forms of brain disease are accompanied by profound depression and continuous disorientation.

Chest

Problems in the lungs and the upper respiratory system are accompanied by coughing and shortness of breath. The most common illnesses are pneumonia and kennel cough, an infection which is the canine equivalent of the common cold. An affected dog is often depressed and off its food.

Kennel cough gets its name from the fact that it is often caught in boarding kennels, where the animal is in close contact with other dogs, and it results in inflammation of the back of the throat and the top of the windpipe. The illness is generally overcome by the dog's immune system if the invading bacteria are of the *Streptococcus* group. But if *Bordetella* bacteria invade the inflamed tissue, the coughing symptoms simulate whooping cough in humans, and the sound of the coughing can be quite alarming, even though it is rarely life-threatening. It is normally treated with antibiotics. Vaccination against kennel cough can be included in a dog's regular annual vaccination. With so many dogs now living in the suburbs, in close proximity to each other, you frequently find dogs with kennel cough who have never been to a kennel. Hence the modern name 'canine cough'.

Ears
The ear canal should always be clear pink to grey, with no discharge or signs of inflammation, and no smell. An ear problem is usually indicated by redness, irritation, an obvious discharge of pus and/or black wax, and an offensive odour. In severe cases a dog will indicate the problem by tilting its head to one side, constantly shaking the head, and scratching the affected ear.

Eyes
A dog with an upset eye, or surrounds of the eye, will have closed eyelids, excess tears, and sometimes a pus discharge. The eye will frequently be a source of

irritation, and the dog will rub it with its paw. Because of the complex nature of the eye, all conditions of the eye should be considered an emergency.

Senile cataracts can occur in dogs of 10 or more years old, and they are diagnosed by a cloudy, later turning silvery, colour behind the pupil. These cataracts can be removed if both eyes are affected and the dog is threatened with blindness, but this is usually only done for younger dogs.

Heart

Most heart problems are associated with degenerative disease, and the onset is slow. Difficulties are first noticed when a dog lacks exercise energy, and even though it's enthusiastic about going for a walk, it will suddenly stop and go no further. Other symptoms are shortness of breath, coughing at the slightest exertion and gradual loss of body condition.

Mouth

Problems are usually indicated by drooling, and the excessive production of saliva, or by a fierce halitosis (bad breath). Dogs drooling suggests they have a foreign body stuck somewhere in the oral cavity, or a decayed tooth has become loosened, or they have suffered an injury to some part of the mouth, like the tongue. Before rushing to the vet, *look*!

There are three main causes of halitosis. The first is a problem in the mouth, and this is usually one or more decayed teeth. The second is odour emanating from the stomach and the upper intestines, and, while this could indicate a serious internal illness, it usually means the dog has eaten something highly smelly, or has been fed on a diet causing halitosis. If it's caused by diet, the smell will be stronger immediately after eating, and then fade away after meals. The third, and least frequent cause, is problems stemming from the respiratory system.

Nose

The nose should always be clean, and without discharge, so the appearance of blood or pus requires prompt examination. The airways should always be clear. The old saying that a wet nose is the sign of a healthy dog is only partially true. Dogs go through a cyclical pattern where their nose is cold and wet, then warm and wet, followed by warm and dry, and cold and dry. When a dog's nose is consistently warm and dry, this indicates that something is wrong.

Reproductive system

Any discharge of blood or pus from the vulva must be investigated. In a bitch that has not been desexed, this usually indicates problems with the uterus. If a bitch is pregnant, any green-coloured discharge indicates she has gone into labour and there is difficulty in the birth of a puppy.

Any swelling of the testicles in a dog that has not been desexed must be investigated, as should the prostate of all older males which have not been desexed and that are having problems defecating.

Skeletal problems

These are commonly caused by the failure of bones to develop correctly, or by degenerative joint and bone disease. If either of these are seen in a limb, the most obvious sign will be lameness. Alternatively, if the condition exists in the spinal column, it is likely to show as weakness in the fore or hind quarters, inability to jump up, and crying out if the sore area is touched, or when the dog moves, particularly at night, or when it gets up in the morning.

Most bone development diseases are inherited. One of the more common, osteochondrosis dissecans, is a failure of the elbow or shoulder joints to develop correctly, and it causes persistent front-leg lameness. Hip dysplasia affects the ball and socket joints causing gait problems, lameness and weak hindquarters.

Degenerative bone disease, which is known as osteoarthritis, occurs in many breeds through a genetic susceptibility, or as a result of trauma earlier in the dog's life. Some dogs have a poorly engineered spinal column, and eventually the body breaks down under the excessive pressures placed on bones and joints. Spinal disc problems, for example, are commonly seen in Dachshunds, Pekingese, Beagles, Australian Terriers, and Cavalier King Charles Spaniels. The disc acts like cushions between the bones, but when the disc becomes inflamed and damaged the cushion function is lost, and the bones rub together causing acute pain.

Dogs are just as prone to lower back problems as humans. The larger breeds, such as Labradors, Retrievers, Dobermanns, Rottweilers and Airedales, are all susceptible to osteoarthritis in this area, and it is frequently seen after the age of eight. In other dogs, osteoarthritis may be brought on by an injury such as being hit by a motor vehicle.

Skin

Dermatitis is the second most common reason after vaccination for owners bringing their dogs to a vet. Nearly all skin complaints are characterised by irritation, accompanied by scratching and hair loss, signs of redness and inflammation and, in untreated cases, infection. Regardless of the type of dermatitis, the dog will have a body odour.

The most frequent dermatitis is allergic dermatitis, which is commonly seen during warm, dry weather, when there are more allergens around. The four main sources of these allergens are fleas, inhaled allergens, vegetation and food.

The most common food allergic reaction is to beef protein. Most dogs are not allergic to fish protein or chicken, although you will find isolated cases where dogs do react.

Allergic reactions to vegetation can cause two sorts of dermatitis in dogs. The first is from direct contact of the skin with a particular sap of a creeper or grass, and the second is caused by the dog inhaling the reproductive pollen of the plant. As with hay fever in humans, this form of vegetative dermatitis is usually seasonal. Couch grass and paspalum are the two grasses that most commonly provoke a reaction, while Wandering Jew

(*Trandescantia* spp.) often irritates dogs' skin. Pollen from the wattle (*Acacia* spp.) can upset many dogs.

Parasites, like mites and ticks, and hormonal deficiencies are also common causes of dermatitis (see pp. 130–132).

Cancer

Superficial cancers, which occur on the surface of the skin, or just beneath it, are the most easily identified because they form noticeable lumps, or sores which don't heal. The lumps that are clearly defined, soft, loosely attached and slow growing are usually benign. Those that are irregular in shape, hard, and growing rapidly, are almost certainly malignant. All cancers that have reached the stage of ulceration to the surface are malignant.

Internal cancers are just as difficult to diagnose in dogs as they are in humans. There are no specific tests for tumours in dogs, and the diagnosis is done by the elimination of possibilities, by locating an unusual lump in the abdomen, or by recognising an unusual mass on an X-ray. Breeds that are most susceptible to internal cancers include Boxers, German Shepherds, and terriers.

Consulting your vet

If you notice any of the above warning signs of illness or injury in your dog, you should consult your vet. The vet will take a history of the complaint, and after conducting a full clinical examination, will make a provisional diagnosis of which system of the body is affected, and what the specific problem is. Wherever necessary, a provisional diagnosis is followed by tests, to confirm the diagnosis, and to ascertain the likely outcome of treatment.

Vets can use two alternative methods of treatment: medical or surgical. Medical treatment consists of the use of specific drugs to augment the body's own healing system. For instance, the function of antibiotics is to kill bacteria that overpower the body's defence system. Surgery is used to repair damaged tissue, such as a broken bone, or to remove diseased tissue, such as a tumour, or foreign objects which may have been swallowed by the dog. Where the surgery is likely to be complex, a veterinary general practitioner will refer the case to a specialist.

When I first went into practice in Balwyn, one out of every two pups that I vaccinated would be killed within a year in motor vehicle accidents. Hardly a day went by without treating a serious car accident victim. A large number died, and a large number of those that survived had fractures. Nowadays, most of the dog-owning public understands the undesirability of their animals being hit by a motor vehicle, and I only see a couple of cases a year. We've come a long way, and there's no doubt owners have become more responsible. For the animals that do still get hit by cars, and suffer broken bones, the prognosis is generally excellent.

MEDICAL ADVANCES

There has been an explosion of knowledge in veterinary science since the mid-1960s, with medical and surgical advances matched by a huge development in pharmaceuticals. When I graduated there were only two antibiotics available, and now there is a vast range, with quite specific applications for particular conditions. There are better painkilling drugs for osteoarthritis, giving quicker, long-lasting relief, and safer anaesthetics have removed the risk from many surgical procedures. We have reached the point where the only barrier to the medical and surgical treatment of dogs is expense. Of course we can do kidney transplants on dogs, but who's going to pay up to $50,000?

In a practice which treats companion animals, people are purchasing veterinary services with recreational dollars, and the work done by the practitioner depends on the availability of those recreational dollars. In difficult economic times, the much-loved family pet won't always receive the ideal treatment. In my practice during the last recession I saw dogs coming in with diseases which would have been prevented if the owners had been able to afford the proper preventative treatment. In many cases owners did not replace the animals they lost.

DON'T DELAY TREATMENT

It is essential that owners do not delay the seeking of treatment when they notice that something is wrong with their dog. Delaying treatment often means the condition is allowed to deteriorate, and this can entail more expensive treatment, or owners may find the animal has reached the point where treatment can no longer be successful. Owners recognise the warning signs quicker these days than they did 30 years ago, but we still see acute cases where the severity of the situation has not been recognised.

Look beyond the immediate symptoms. A dog suffering from a primary upset bowel or stomach will usually experience short-term diarrhoea or vomiting, but the dog is generally bright and alert. If the symptoms continue and the dog is not bright and alert, it is usually a sign of something more sinister. Assess the whole of the dog's condition and state of mind, or you may misinterpret its real condition.

Often I see dogs that are quite sick where the owner will explain away the illness as being caused by the weather, or something the dog has eaten. Animals do not speak, but they also do not hide what is wrong with them. While dogs may accommodate pain and suffering because they can't ask for veterinary treatment, they never disguise what's wrong.

It is dangerous to make your own interpretation or diagnosis of your dog's condition. A lady came in to see me with a dog that had its left eye swollen and closed. She had decided that the dog had been stung by a bee, and that it would get better by itself. She went to work early the next day, and when she got home the following evening she noticed that the swelling was much worse, and that there was a stream of tears and some pus discharge between the eyelids. The dog was in considerable distress.

When I examined the dog I found there had been a penetration through the cornea and an infection had been introduced and it had become so acute that the dog's sight had been destroyed. Antibiotics cleared up the infection but ultimately the eye had to be removed. Had treatment been given earlier, the sight may not have been saved, but the eye would have been.

In another case I saw a three-year-old terrier which was losing hair on both flanks. The owners had correctly observed that the hair was slowly thinning, and that the problem was not accompanied by scratching. They delayed coming to me because they'd decided the dog was pulling its hair out by scratching itself underneath the car. It was only when the hair had fully dropped out, revealing two large bald patches, that they sought my advice.

When I diagnosed the condition as thyroid hormonal baldness they refused to accept the diagnosis because they believed the dog was self-mutilating. The dog grew its hair again, but the delay in seeking this diagnosis meant many months of treatment were needed.

An elderly lady brought in a little Dachshund because the dog was coughing. It turned out the dog had been coughing for three months and it clearly had respiratory distress and was lethargic. The owner admitted that the dog had been getting worse over the past three months, and no longer wanted to go for its usual daily walk. She and her housekeeper had decided the dog had a cold, but it was only when it became much worse that they sought my advice.

Examination of the dog revealed that it was suffering from left heart failure, and the coughing, breathing problems and the lack of interest in food and exercise were all due to the fact that the dog's lungs were seriously affected by a fluid build-up due to the heart failure. Very little of the lung tissue was functioning normally, and the dog was severely starved of oxygen.

I expressed the view that the dog would not respond well to heart treatment, but fortunately the response to a newly released drug for cardiac therapy proved amazing. The issue, though, is how long will a drug keep sustaining a dog with a badly damaged heart?

Another case involved a young Labrador with pancreatitis, where the delay in treatment could have cost the dog's life. The pancreas, like the brain and kidneys, does not regenerate even after successful treatment, so once it is damaged, it is damaged for life. The dog had been vomiting for five days, was depressed, and not eating. It took four days of intensive treatment before I was sure that the dog would live. It survived, but great damage had been done to the pancreas, and the dog is now required to live on a special diet, together with supplementary pancreatic enzymes. The owner said it had eaten something that disagreed with it.

The cardinal rule is that if the dog vomits for more than 12 hours, go to the vet. Sometimes people delay going to the vet because of the expense, but most of it is due to ignorance, backed by a belief that the animal will get better by itself. Plenty of people believe in soldiering on; some even don't come because they're afraid Dr Wirth will roar at them!

A minority, when confronted by their own failure to be responsible, put the blame on the vet by saying, 'You never told me to do that.' I've even been blamed for a dog being involved in a car accident, because I never warned the owner the dog might get out.

People are often keen to seek a 'quick fix' for their dog from the vet. The veterinarian should provide advice on dog welfare issues, and rapid diagnosis of all health problems, followed by medical and surgical treatment. But the primary responsibility for the health and welfare of a dog lies fairly and squarely with its owner. It's their responsibility to feed and house the dog, but also to recognise when the dog is not well, and to then seek advice. The emphasis in dog ownership is always that prevention is better than a cure. We live in an age where there is an abundance of information about dog care, and there's no excuse for the continuance of old myths, supposition, and conjecture.

4

Dogs in the community

THE FIGHT FOR DOGS' RIGHTS

My first exposure to cruelty to dogs came when I was a child, through the Australian and Silky Terriers that were bred by the woman who lived next to us in Ivanhoe. The breeder's daughter broke up a long-standing romance with her boyfriend, and he came back one night through the paddock where we kept our Shetland pony and threw strychnine baits into the runs of the dogs, to exact revenge on the girlfriend who had jilted him. In the morning the breeder found most of her dogs were dead, including her champion show dog. It was the first of many occasions when I have seen a human problem resolved by making innocent animals the victim.

Professionally, I came head-to-head with animal cruelty for the first time when I was a 22-year-old, fourth-year veterinary student, and I have never forgotten it. I was spending time doing work experience with the Balwyn veterinary practice which I now own, and one of the vets there, who regularly did work for the RSPCA, was called to attend a case of suspected cruelty at a farmhouse in Doncaster. All we knew was that the woman had dogs, but when we went into the house we were confronted by room after room containing dogs in tea chests with grilles on the front. The chests were stacked one on top of the other, and they contained 45 dogs, all of which were suffering from distemper or starvation. Most had to be put down.

In my view, the woman wasn't mentally sound, as is the case with all animal hoarders, and like so many of the cruelty cases involving neglect which I have subsequently been involved with, she couldn't explain why she neglected the animals.

I felt intense anger as I helped the vet destroy the dogs and then dumped all the bodies outside for the council to pick up. There had to be something wrong if we had to slaughter all these animals, and I kept asking myself, why weren't the dogs vaccinated, and why couldn't the RSPCA have prevented their suffering? I'm a veterinarian, and I believe the principles of veterinary science can improve the health and wellbeing of animals, but at that moment I was suddenly exposed to the fact that veterinary science had done absolutely nothing for those 45 dogs in tea chests. This was one of the defining moments in my veterinary career.

When I was at school at Xavier College we had been taught the importance of doing work for the community, and each week I used to go and help the down-and-outs. From the time I was 14 I felt with growing conviction that my community work would be for animals. The feeling strengthened when I went to veterinary school in Brisbane, and the lecturers instilled in the students the idea that veterinarians were professional people with an obligation to the community. Incidents like the one at the farmhouse in Doncaster all had an influence on me, and from the time I went onto the RSPCA (Victoria) Board in 1969, I was determined that the principles of veterinary science would be used by the RSPCA to prevent the death of animals. There was something evangelistic about it: I believed I had the answers to help animals, and I wanted to tell people.

The problem of strays

When I became a vet the public mainly saw the issue of cruelty in terms of overt cruelty, which meant the infliction of pain and suffering on an animal by a human. It was some time before the covert cruelty of neglect, such as confining animals to cages, or the subtleties of starvation, came to the fore. When I commenced practice in Melbourne the major issue with dogs was how strays were rounded up and handled in the public pounds and, ultimately, how they were destroyed. The prevailing attitude was that stray dogs were little better than vermin; they were nuisance animals that had to be taken off the streets and got rid of as quickly as possible.

Much of the pressure to deal with strays fell on the Lost Dogs' Home in North Melbourne, which had been founded in 1910 as a charitable institution to 'help lost, strayed, sick or injured animals who, for any reason, have no human being who will help them in their distress'. In 1913 the Home had taken in 1400 dogs, but by the late 1970s it was having to accommodate up to 27,000 dogs a year in facilities that were by now antiquated and inadequate. In one extreme circumstance they had to accept 700 in one day.

When I first visited the Lost Dogs' Home in 1965 it had a huge impact on me. The buildings were in decay, the pens were crowded, and there was no application of veterinary science. Dogs were not vaccinated on entry, and whilst things were kept clean, there was no routine application of disinfectant. They were doing a good job with limited resources, but I knew that if veterinary science principles had been adopted there would be a great improvement in the quality of the lives of the animals. The thing that angered me was the attitude of not treating the dogs on entry because they were strays, and therefore second-class animals, and why spend money on those that were about to die anyway?

There had also been growing public concern about the euthanasia methods used at the Home. Until natural gas was introduced to Melbourne in 1969, the dogs that could not be adopted were destroyed in a gas chamber. Later a decompression chamber was introduced, which worked by denying oxygen to the dogs, who then blacked out after four minutes. The RSPCA pressed successfully for the dogs to be destroyed individually, with a barbiturate injection, which is now the current practice in all shelters.

Being confronted with the conditions at the Lost Dogs' Home committed me to the need for changes in the governance of the RSPCA, so that we could establish new standards for the treatment of stray animals. The RSPCA at that time did not have kennels, and as soon as dogs came in, they would be sent off to the Lost Dogs' Home. I knew we needed to introduce an animal hospital and shelter at the RSPCA's Victorian headquarters in Burwood, and I was fortunate to have a Board and chief executive officer who supported me.

PART 4 DOGS IN THE COMMUNITY

Around 1980 the RSPCA in Victoria was handling about 10,000 animals annually, and it did so without the benefit of any in-house veterinary service to treat the animals. I proposed that a veterinary clinic ought to be established at Burwood with resident employed staff, and when word reached the Australian Veterinary Association (AVA), and in particular the Melbourne practitioners, they began lobbying the RSPCA Board on the grounds that the clinic would be uneconomic, and would duplicate services that were already available. What they didn't say was that the establishment of an RSPCA clinic would bring unwarranted competition to veterinary practitioners.

They put up alternatives, but these all foundered because it was glaringly obvious that the various schemes weren't based on the belief that stray, sick and injured dogs had exactly the same rights to proper veterinary care as animals belonging to fee-paying private clients. Most of the schemes they proposed involved outside vets treating the animals after they had looked after their own clients. We said the strays had equal priority, and must be attended to without delay.

It was a watershed for the RSPCA and the AVA. For the first time the veterinary profession was forced to consider whether stray animals deserved the same standard of veterinary treatment as normally owned animals, or whether they should remain second-class animals. Veterinarians had to face up to their professional obligations, and whether they should expect a fee for everything they did. They also had to confront the first guiding principle of the AVA's Code of Ethics, which states that 'the primary concern of the veterinary profession is for the welfare of animals'.

All we wanted to do was relieve the suffering of sick and injured dogs, and we found ourselves opposed by the veterinary practitioners of Melbourne. The veterinary profession was telling me there would be no RSPCA clinic in Melbourne. I'm quite capable of reaching a compromise, and I've had to negotiate many during my time as RSPCA president since 1972, but I will never accept an organisation laying down the law to me.

I could have understood the opposition if it had been confined to an individual group of vets with a practice next door to the RSPCA clinic, and who feared the impact on their livelihood. The RSPCA Board had tried to overcome this kind of concern by issuing a directive that the primary obligation of the clinic was the care of animals committed to the RSPCA, and that no RSPCA vet was to engage in private practice unless the needs of all the animals in the care of the RSPCA had been met.

The shelter and an accompanying veterinary clinic opened in February 1981 and when animals came in they were given a full veterinary examination, wormed, treated for any illnesses, and prepared for adoption or, alternatively, a humane death. The RSPCA also encouraged the government to introduce a code of practice for pounds and shelters. It also discouraged the use of shelter dogs for live animal experimentation.

The opening of the RSPCA clinic at the Burwood shelter caused a bitter and long-lasting conflict with many of my veterinary colleagues, who had lobbied to stop the clinic opening because it might affect their own practices. It caused a collision between the RSPCA and the AVA that was not resolved for many years, and which led to my being ostracised by the AVA, and dumped from the position of AVA honorary federal secretary.

Even today, 30 years later, many individual veterinarians still oppose the clinic and will not assist the RSPCA in any way. In my view, the response of some of my colleagues suggested they had little appreciation of the rights of animals, and their attitude seemed to be governed by factors other than animal welfare. I felt they were acting more like a trade union than a profession. The animosities built up over that issue have never been forgotten.

Animals need our support

I had always had strong feelings for animals, to the point where, in my younger days, friends and family sometimes accused me of ignoring the natural order, and putting animals before humans. I wasn't ignoring the natural order, it was just that I preferred working with animals. I spoke for those who could not speak for themselves. The issue for me was that animals needed more protection than they had, and they needed vocal support from people who made a living from them, which included veterinarians.

Some veterinarians agreed with my views but thought they were impractical, and that I was forgetting where veterinarians derived their income. My attitude was that if I was going to be the animals' advocate, I had to be the advocate, come what may. There is a terror among some of my colleagues that if you speak up, you will lose income, and I'm sure I have. No-one comes to Hugh Wirth any more to get their dogs' tails cut off, and how much income have I lost over that?

Apart from the issue of the treatment of strays by RSPCA vets, the general welfare of dogs did not cause much conflict within the veterinary profession. Dogs have a favoured position in the animal pecking order, and affection for this animal transcends all social classes and groupings. They've displaced the horse in the affection of Australians, and they are loved equally by workers and directors, town and country people.

The tail-docking debate

From 1980, part of the RSPCA's strategy for making the organisation more relevant to the community has been to publish policy statements on the justified and acceptable use of animals by humans. Two of these policies, desexing and tail-docking, brought us into fierce conflict with dog breeders.

Up to that point, the community had tended to the view that animals could be adapted or modified to suit humans, but the RSPCA was now questioning the right of humans to make those changes which were not essential for the animal's welfare. It had become accepted practice that breeders cut off the tails of dogs like Rottweilers, Cocker Spaniels, Boxers, and German Short-haired Pointers, and the rules of showing certain breeds even demanded that the dogs tails' be docked. The RSPCA anti-docking campaign eventually triumphed — on 1 April 2004 the docking of dogs' tails for purely cosmetic purposes was made a criminal offence throughout Australia.

The desexing debate

Throughout the world one of the major animal welfare problems is that of the stray dog. How this problem is dealt with varies from culture to culture and in many cases the suffering endured by stray dogs is compounded by the cruelty used to capture these dogs and euthanase them.

The obvious answer is to limit the number of dogs born with the ultimate aim that all puppies born will be placed in a good home and enjoy a fulfilling life. In Australia the RSPCA believes that all dogs that are to be kept as pets, whether male or female, should be compulsorily desexed before puberty.

The benefits that accrue from desexing are not limited to prevention of reproduction. There are many health issues that do not occur in dogs that have been desexed, and often behaviour is greatly modified, especially in male dogs.

To emphasise the gravity of the situation facing the RSPCA shelter network, in 2008–2009 the RSPCA alone nationally admitted to its shelters 69,383 dogs of which 22,896 were reclaimed by owners and 19,236 were adopted. The remaining 22,085 were euthanased. RSPCA (Victoria) figures for the same period were dog admissions 18,116, reclaimed 8846, adopted 4939 and euthanased 3958. The figures are far worse for cats.

Politicians are loath to enact legislation requiring the compulsory desexing of pets, leaving the issue to be decided at the municipal level. Those municipalities that have enacted local laws on compulsory desexing have usually limited the legislation to the desexing of cats. The Australian Veterinary Association is opposed to compulsory desexing of pet animals stating that this will not reduce excess numbers of animals.

The AVA does not offer a viable alternative action that will assist animal welfare groups in dramatically slashing the current shelter euthanasia rates.

The debate is not limited to compulsory desexing, but includes a quasi-academic argument on when to desex. For obvious reasons the RSPCA will not adopt out any dog that has not been desexed and this often means desexing puppies as early as eight weeks of age. There is no published scientific work that suggests that early age desexing causes later problems. Whenever I am faced with argument from my veterinary colleagues on this matter I am reminded of a survey of British veterinarians on the question of when is the best time to desex a pet animal. The winning response was 'At 11 am straight after morning tea'.

Animal hoarding

Many of us will remember growing up in new suburbs on the edge of rural areas and can recall local people living alone with a great many dogs or cats. These people were always reclusive and were living in very poorly kept habitation.

Nowadays we recognise these people as having

a mental illness resulting in them becoming animal hoarders. They have no capacity to look after the large number of animals that they accumulate and in fact they are incapable of acknowledging that the animals are suffering from their neglect.

Resolving the issue is difficult. Many of the animals rescued from such a situation are in practical terms not able to be rehabilitated. Co-ordinating all of the various authorities to assist resolution is not easy as the mental health condition is not well recognised. Recidivism is almost 100 per cent. Simply prosecuting the person responsible for the animal cruelty solves nothing. Better surveillance at the local level to ensure discovery of animal hoarding at an early stage is essential. The Victorian Domestic Animals Act limits the ownership of dogs to two unless a permit is granted to own a larger number.

Puppy farms

Puppy breeding establishments take many forms and can be seen to be a continuum from extremely bad (puppy farms, exploitive hoarders) through to excellent (dog enthusiasts who put the animals' health and welfare as the first priority).

Puppy farming is the indiscriminate breeding of dogs on a large scale for the purposes of sale. Puppy farms, also known as puppy mills or puppy factories, are essentially commercial operations with an emphasis on production and profit with little or no consideration given to the welfare of the animals. Puppy farms are intensive systems with breeding animals and their puppies kept in facilities that fail to meet the animals' psychological, behavioural, social or physiological needs. As a result of a failure to meet acceptable animal welfare standards many of these animals have a poor quality of life. Puppy farming and animal hoarding are generally considered to be different phenomena based on the owner's motivation for having the animals. However, in many ways the results can be similar — a large number of animals kept in extremely poor conditions.

Once again poorly worded legislation, together with poor enforcements standards, permits puppy farms to develop without being accountable for the suffering and cruelty that occurs.

Dumping is an offence

Although there has been a dramatic shift in community attitudes to cruelty in the last 20 years the fact is that we still permit the over-breeding, and therefore the oversupply, of puppies for which there are not sufficient homes available. Many of us continue to wrongly select a puppy and, having done so, fail to educate and train it so that it becomes a valued pet. We blame the dog for these failings, never ourselves, and think nothing of getting rid of it at the first available opportunity. Dumping the dog out of a car in a remote area, or simply allowing the dog to take its chances by wandering off via a deliberately left open back gate, is recognised as a cruel act throughout Australia. The unwanted dog could have easily been surrendered at an RSPCA shelter with few questions asked, so why does dumping still happen?

PART 4 DOGS IN THE COMMUNITY

Since 1990 I have seen the number of dogs entering the RSPCA Victorian shelters plateau to around 20,000 per year. Despite a range of initiatives, including changes to the law, this figure remains stubbornly predictable. I acknowledge that there is a great deal more work to be done in educating the community to recognise and do something about their general lack of skills in dog ownership. I believe dog ownership is a privilege, not a right, and further that all dog owners should be licensed as a fit and proper person to own a dog rather than continue with the old system of dog licensing.

Dumping animals is a criminal offence under the State and Territory Prevention of Cruelty to Animals Acts, which provides a fine of $12,000 or one year's imprisonment for a first offence.

Violence towards dogs

There is still a clear tendency for people to vent their frustrations by 'kicking the dog'. Research has shown that violence against animals rises in proportion to the general level of violence within the community. When you have a violent society, more violence is directed against dogs or other animals.

I remember a harrowing example of that cruelty, reported in April 1995 in a front page article in *The Age* under the headline 'Dog's three-day ordeal ends in death'. The case involved a Jack Russell Terrier, kept in a flat in the Melbourne suburb of Prahran, which had been stabbed through the throat with a screwdriver. This followed three days of beating and kicking which left the dog with broken ribs. The investigating RSPCA inspector said the killing was 'beyond comprehension', and described it as the worst case of cruelty he had witnessed in 13 years as an inspector.

Neighbours told police they heard the sound of a dog yelping coming from the flat for three days, and the autopsy revealed that the dog had been kicked over successive days, cracking ribs, and causing a punctured lung. It had then had food rammed down its throat with a foot-long Philips-head screwdriver, causing its liver to be ruptured and resulting in its death.

The inspector said the killing was more disturbing as it was not a frenzied one-off attack, but the result of accumulated episodes of cruelty over three days. He said that while this was an extreme case, there appeared to be a perception that pets could be used as punching bags for owners to vent their frustrations.

The dog's owner, a 27-year-old man, was charged under the Prevention of Cruelty to Animals Act with aggravated cruelty. At that time the charge carried penalties of up to 12 months in jail or a $5000 fine (now $24,000 or two years imprisonment).

It was a case of barbaric cruelty and one of about 15,000 complaints received each year by the RSPCA. The organisation has always fought against such overt cruelty, but since becoming Victorian president in 1972 I have also campaigned to stop the covert cruelty of owner ignorance and irresponsibility. Often owners inflict pain and suffering simply by not understanding their dog, or by putting themselves first. A good officer always looks after his troops, and that's the way it is with dogs: the good dog owner always considers the animal first. If you take on another part of creation, you're obliged to look after it.

Kindness can be cruelty

I have tried to change the attitudes of people who buy a dog as a fashionable play thing, to be turned on and off as required; or those people who kill the dog with kindness, by feeding it till it can't move; or those owners who hold on to the dog well beyond its use-by date.

OBESITY

In 2000 a survey of companion animal veterinary practices was conducted by the RSPCA and the University of Sydney Faculty of Veterinary Science to determine the prevalence of overweight and obesity in dogs. The results were:

- 41 per cent of dogs surveyed were found to be overweight or obese, 55 per cent ideal and only 4 per cent underweight;
- Dogs are more likely to encounter weight problems than any other companion animal;
- Animals at greater risk are female, desexed, older, poorly exercised, with obese owners;
- The survey figures duplicated similar results of surveys in the UK and the USA.

Owners will often argue that it is cruelty to deny the dog titbits, particularly if the dog is present while the owner is eating. The action is often rationalised with the belief that giving the dog a little bit of biscuit won't really hurt, but this goes against all the accumulated evidence of human experience. You're overweight because you eat too much and don't exercise enough. Excuses that the dog is fat because it's desexed, or because of a glandular problem, are a plain denial of the truth, and a sure sign that the owner has no intention of taking responsibility for the health problems resulting from the fact that the animal is chronically overweight.

So many conditions are caused or exacerbated by being overweight. Obesity has been proven to be a factor in diabetes, heart disorders and Cushing's disease (a condition of the adrenal gland), and it also causes discomfort to dogs with degenerative spinal diseases, because they are carrying too much weight. Elderly dogs often won't exercise because their weight problem makes it difficult for them to get around. There is no doubt such a dog suffers misery, but the proper word to describe it is cruelty.

THE DECISION TO PUT YOUR DOG DOWN

Putting a dog down is a very emotional act for anyone, however resigned they might have become to its inevitability. The general rule is that if a dog cannot, through medical or surgical treatment, be returned to a situation where it can once again enjoy life, then, ethically, it should be put down. It's cruelty to delay doing so, and it is usually based on an act of personal indulgence, coupled with a refusal to submit oneself to the inevitable pain and anguish associated with the loss of a dog.

The decision to end a dog's life is usually clear-cut when the animal has suffered some acute medical problem or a serious traumatic injury, but it's much less obvious in the many degenerative diseases suffered by dogs. In an acute situation, the owner is guided by the vet, but in the chronic degenerative cases, while the vet's advice is essential, it is up to the owner to decide how far he or she is prepared to allow the condition to progress.

These guidelines will help an owner make the best decision:

- The dog can no longer walk — there is nothing more distressing to a dog than to lack mobility.
- The dog is unable to consume sufficient food on a daily basis to prevent loss of bodyweight.
- The dog's lack of hearing or eyesight frequently places it in life-threatening situations.
- The dog is clearly in constant pain.
- The dog has become incontinent (bowel or bladder).
- The dog no longer reacts positively to its environment, or to the day-to-day happenings involving interaction with humans. It has become vegetative, simply existing between feeds.

Once a decision has been made that a dog has lost all its quality of life, the dog must be put down without delay. The wise owner will have held a conference with all family members involved in the decision, so that everyone is well aware of the situation. When the time comes, all these people should attend the veterinary surgeon with the dog, and be physically present in some way, holding the dog when the injection is given.

It's a matter of personal choice whether the dog is buried at home, or left with the vet to be disposed of by burial or cremation. I have always believed that burying dogs in the back yard has often delayed the ending of a mourning period, and the act of replacement with a new dog. It can also lead to emotional problems if the dog's remains have to be left behind if the home is sold. A mourning period is essential to the recovery after the loss of the dog, because it enables one's memory of the dog to be put in to perspective, and it permits the ownership of a new dog.

Ensuring the dog has a dignified death is the final part of the contract of responsibility which the owner enters into when he first purchases the dog. We've domesticated all these animals, we've brought them into the world, we've purchased them, and we have an obligation to look after them, right up to and including their death.

WHEN THE LAW BITES

Dog ownership was never a problem 40 years ago; we fed them; we took them for walks; we brought them home; and we did it all without aggravation. Today dogs have become a major issue, and the community is divided between the dog lobby and the anti-dog lobby. The force of the law now hovers above dog owners who take their dog for a walk in the park without a leash. What has happened since the early 1960s?

The answer is that we have far more dogs and we have changed as a community, and in the way we keep our dogs. When I began practising as a vet in Balwyn in 1965 there wasn't another veterinary practice for another 20 kilometres in the direction of Melbourne's outer eastern suburbs. Today, in response to the growing numbers of dogs, there are veterinary practices all over the place.

Lifestyles have changed since 1965 when Mum was always home to look after the dog. Today we have moved into the gentrified inner-city areas, with backyards the size of a postage stamp, and Mum has gone out to work, leaving the dog all alone. The stresses and isolation of modern life can cause people to want the comfort of a dog more than ever, but even though we only have enough space to keep a Chihuahua, we buy a Cattle Dog or a Rottweiler, because they are fashionable. Then we find that they bark from separation anxiety when we leave to go to work, or they snarl at someone in the park. The council ranger gets called, and suddenly the dog becomes an issue involving the law. The dog gets blamed, but the dog hasn't changed in the past 40 years; we're the ones who've changed.

Dog owners only have themselves to blame. They have bought the wrong type of dog, confined them in inappropriate urban settings, and failed to give them proper training and socialisation. The resulting problems of roaming, barking and dog attacks have left governments with little alternative but to produce a more comprehensive dog legislation. The law will always respond when an overwhelming need for action arises, as it has done with dog ownership.

Dog attacks

There is no lack of evidence of problems associated with dogs. With increasing regularity we are reading the newspaper headline 'Dog Mauls Boy In Park'. The owner may always forgive the misbehaviour of their dog, but when private failings turn to public terror, the law will not exhibit the same indulgence to owner and animal.

In 1988 the Victorian Parliament was told that there had been 6000 reported incidents involving humans or other animals being bitten by dogs during the course of the previous year. These attacks ranged from surface scratches to severe maulings requiring hospitalisation and surgery. Evidence from police, local councils and hospitals suggests that the level of these incidents has been consistent over the period 1987–2010, with reported dog bites rising by 10 per cent per annum.

Though there have been numerous cases since, I distinctly recall an incident that was reported on the front page of the *Sunday Age* on 21 May 1995. It involved the common elements of a young child, an apparently irresponsible owner, and a breed of dog with an instinctive tendency to attack if uncontrolled. An eight-year-old schoolboy had been playing in a park in South Yarra, accompanied by an adult after-school assistant, when he was mauled by an English Bull Terrier. The newspaper reported that the attack came after the 21-year-old owner of the dog let the animal off the leash for exercise, despite the fact that there were signs in the park requiring dogs to be kept on leashes at all times. The dog then went up to a group of school children which included the eight-year-old boy. The police officer handling the case said, 'The kids were playing with the dog but the boy got scared. He screamed and ran away and then the dog, it seems, has chased and mauled him.'

The boy recovered after undergoing surgery. The owner of the Bull Terrier was charged with two offences under the 1970 Dog Act.

A few days after that case was reported I was notified of another attack involving a Bull Terrier, this time on a Jack Russell. The Bull Terrier had been muzzled, but when it saw the other dog in a Melbourne park, it charged over and attacked the animal. The dog's muzzle came off in the attack, and the Jack Russell suffered injuries requiring over $350 worth of veterinary treatment. When the melee had died down the Bull Terrier's owner appeared, carrying the animal's lead.

I regard it as the height of irresponsibility to let a dog off the lead when the owner knows the animal is violent, even if the owner has placed a muzzle on the dog to curb its aggression. I believe the dog problem won't be solved until you crack down on owners.

The off-leash dog has become more and more of a problem with other dogs and humans. The ideal dog is under voice control, but in practice, very few dogs are under this type of control, despite what their owners think. Few dogs can resist responding to their basic instincts, and even fewer will resist being distracted by another animal. Even the best voice-controlled dog will find it almost impossible to resist chasing a cat or a fluffy dog.

Australia has a continuing problem with irresponsible dog owners who refuse to accept that they have a social responsibility to ensure that their dog behaves. Owners are blind to the anti-social behaviour of their dog, just as parents are often blind to the faults of their children, and they won't face up to the fact that as soon as the dog is away from them, and is stimulated by humans or other animals, it bites and becomes uncontrollable. There is a tendency in humans not to want to admit their mistakes, and in this case owners don't like to admit they bought the wrong breed, or failed to train the dog properly. It is all part of the denial process: their dog could never have done what the neighbour or the person on the walk said it did.

WHAT TO DO IF YOU'RE THREATENED

If you are threatened with a dog attack, remember that movement and sound will aggravate a dog which is already excited and proposing to attack. The first thing you must do is come to an absolute halt, and ensure that you are not waving things around — especially an arm or a hand. Remain utterly silent, even if you feel like screaming. Do not stare at the dog. The dog suddenly finds it has nothing to chase, and it will quickly lose interest and will wander off.

AGGRESSIVE BREEDS

Certain breeds are genetically predisposed to aggressive behaviour because of the role they were bred for, and owners should beware that if you switch on the trigger in these animals, they become fighting machines. German Shepherds, Bull Terriers, Dobermanns, Rottweilers and Cattle Dogs consistently appear in reports on dog attacks prepared by local municipalities and health organisations. The old theory was that German Shepherds had to be muzzled because they were savage dogs, and that if they mated with Dingoes it would produce a super-killer of sheep. Until quite recently Western Australia had a regulation that only desexed German Shepherds could enter the state.

A 1991 study by the South Australian Health Commission indicated that German Shepherds, Bull Terriers, Dobermanns, Rottweilers, Cattle Dogs and Collies were responsible for 73 per cent of attacks on adults and children. Another 1991 study, done by rangers from the Melbourne suburb of Frankston, concluded that there were four main types of dog attacks: Cattle Dogs (or Blue Heelers as they are commonly known) were often involved in actual biting attacks; German Shepherds, Dobermanns and Rottweilers featured in rushing attacks; Bull Terriers were generally involved in attacks on other dogs, or cats; and smaller dogs tended to 'nip' out of fear or excitement.

The most recent study (2005–2007) of dog bite attacks on adults and children prepared by the Victorian Injury Surveillance System confirmed the fact that many attacks, 80 per cent, occur in the dog's own home, and frequently on children under the age of five. This was also confirmed by the study of 1093 dog bite injuries to children attending three Melbourne hospitals between 1989 and 1993 which found that 43 per cent of these injuries occurred to toddlers under five, and the most frequent location was outdoors at home.

The extent of the problem was indicated by research conducted in 1992 by the Monash University Accident Research Centre. It found that dog bites to children aged between one and four were a more frequent cause of hospital admission (37 cases per 100,000 people) than either motor vehicle accidents (28 per 100,000) or child maltreatment (12 per 100,000).

The research is consistent: children are more likely to be bitten by their own dog at home, rather than by a strange dog elsewhere, and effort should be put into education for families and children on how to handle dogs.

The main reason children under five get bitten is that they have no fear of dogs, because no-one has taught them the warning signs that a dog is upset and will bite. Invariably the dog is known to the child, who doesn't recognise that the dog has had enough. The animal will growl, and once it has snarled, baring its teeth, it will bite without further warning. Plenty of time is given to educating children on 'stranger danger', but almost none to dog behaviour, and it's because adults don't understand 'dog speak' and the dangers posed by dogs, especially their own.

The Victorian Injury Surveillance System report goes so far as to advocate that people with young children should avoid owning dogs, particularly dangerous breeds. The 1993 Australian Bureau of Statistics home safety survey, which found that 35 per cent of households with young children have dogs, also suggested that families should delay acquiring a dog while the children were under the age of seven.

Nonetheless, despite all of this knowledge about the cause of dog bites and the wide dissemination of this knowledge in the media and through primary schools, I was shocked to learn that in 2009 nine people a week were admitted to Victorian hospitals suffering serious dog bite wounds.

Apart from Queensland, where dog laws are enacted and controlled by local government, all Australian states have a Dog Act, or similar legislation, which specifies how a dog should be kept and controlled. The Act requires that the dog be registered; that it be kept within the owner's property; that it be kept under control when it leaves the owner's property; and that it should not attack humans or other animals.

The Act, which is enforced by local government, is generally perceived as the community's defence against dangerous or troublesome dogs, but it was originally conceived as a way of providing the dog with legal rights. Prior to the Dog Act, dogs were treated as chattels, with no rights, and the new law recognised the dog as a legal entity and set standards for the ownership and control of dogs.

REGISTRATION

Registration is the key to the Dog Act, and once an animal is registered it is protected by the provisions of the Act, and local municipalities are compelled to return it to the owner, should it become lost or separated. The Act imposes a double requirement on the owner to identify the dog. Firstly, it must be registered with the local municipality, but secondly, the dog must carry a marker with the name and address of the owner.

Routine surveys of impounded dogs at this time revealed that no more than 5 per cent of animals were identified according to the law. Owners were registering their dog with the local council, but then they failed to attach either the council's registration marker, or the dog's identity tag.

These tags were the only device we had to connect a dog with its owner. When a dog is hit by a car and suffers a broken leg, and it's brought to me without identity, who do I turn to for permission to go ahead and treat the animal? As a vet, I'm required by the Prevention of Cruelty to Animals Act to relieve the dog's suffering by putting its leg in a splint, but that's as far as I can go without the owner's permission. Often it can take days to find the owner.

Equally frustrating for the RSPCA was the knowledge that most dogs entering its shelters were in reality owned, but without an identity tag that owner could not be traced.

THE IMPORTANCE OF IDENTIFICATION

Murphy's Law operates with dogs. They will get out, despite all the gates and fences you put in their way, and it's a frequent cause of owner distress and dog distress, because the dog doesn't want to be in the pound. It's very depressing when you're running a shelter, and day after day dogs come in with absolutely no identification. All you can do is pray, and hope the owner comes to the pound. If someone is dumping a dog, they will remove all identification, but it's obvious that many dogs who come in are owned.

The development of microchip identification for dogs has dramatically assisted with solving the problem of the unidentified dog. A microchip is inserted under the skin over the left shoulder blade. It contains a unique set of letters and numbers that permanently identifies the dog and these can be read by an electronic scanner which all pound and shelter managers and veterinarians possess. After a period of encouraging dog owners to voluntarily microchip their dogs, legislation was introduced in 2005 making it compulsory for all breeders to microchip puppies prior to sale. At this time microchipping is in addition to the requirement for all dogs to wear their registration marker and owner contact details attached to their collar.

Already the benefit of microchipping is being seen. Most of the dogs separated from their owners in the 2009 Victorian bushfires were eventually returned to their owners, or next of kin, via a microchip.

If people love their dogs as they say they do, why is there still resistance to putting a marker put on them and having them microchipped to link the dog with the owner? It's an utter disgrace, not least because having the dog registered and identified is fundamental to having its rights recognised. The only right for a dog coming into the pound with no identification and no marker is that it will be given eight days before it is put down.

Registration has also been used as a way of encouraging owners to have their animals desexed, as the registration fee for desexed dogs is by law only a third of the fee for animals that have not been desexed. It is intended that the savings on the fee will be equivalent to the cost of having the dog desexed. One benefit of de-sexing an animal is that it becomes more of a 'home body', and therefore less likely to stray, to spread infectious diseases or to be hit by cars.

5

Your dog problems

I have always strongly believed that the key to achieving the full joy of dog ownership lies in understanding as much as is possible to know about dogs. This belief has shaped my approach to veterinary practice and has been one of the reasons for my involvement with the RSPCA.

In 1981 the ABC in Melbourne invited me to be their veterinary expert for a half-hour animal welfare programme. I readily accepted because I felt it would greatly assist me in fulfilling my wish for greater understanding of dogs by their owners. At first, because I was challenging long-held beliefs that were convenient for humans, but did not take into account the needs of the animal, many of my views on the welfare of animals provoked strong listener reaction. I am still saying many of the same things but only rarely is there an angry response, apart from when I talk about correct dog control.

If my talkback segment on 774 is any guide, there has been a dramatic and measurable shift in community attitudes to the welfare of animals in the last 30 years. Yet I find the same questions being repeated each Saturday morning, which suggests to me that it will take many more years at the microphone for owners to fully understand the normal dog, its behaviour and its needs. The following are the most common questions asked by listeners, with the answers I have given on 774, and I include them in the continued hope that owners will strive to understand their dogs.

NEW DOG

House-training

➤ *I have a problem house-training a five-month-old Kelpie cross which I got from the RSPCA two weeks ago. I take her out after eating and sleeping, but when she's inside she goes to the toilet everywhere. How do I train her to stop urinating inside?*

Answer: You have to re-double your efforts because she's past the peak of the learning curve, which is 12 weeks. No puppy can be reliably house-trained under nine months. What you have to do is teach the dog rapidly where to urinate and defecate. I would buy a packet of reward food, so that the dog knows that if it urinates and defecates in front of you in the spot in the garden you've chosen, it will get the reward food.

You shouldn't have the dog in the house for more than 30 minutes without taking it out. If you catch the dog urinating in the house, scold her straight away. If you do it five minutes later, when you find the mark, the dog won't know why it's being punished.

Barking pup

➤ *We have a 15-week-old Groodle which barks at night and annoys the neighbours. What can we do?*

Answer: Your pup has suddenly been forced to spend the night by itself when it has been used to living with its litter mates. Barking is the pup's way of attention seeking. 'Why can't I live with my new human family?' the pup is demanding. You must immediately teach the pup this behaviour is unacceptable. If he is to live outside, then consider confining him to a garage, which will help lower the barking tone. But you must get up every time the pup starts barking and scold him so that he quickly learns that you, the boss dog, will not tolerate barking for no acceptable reason.

Barking at a family member

Our dog has bonded to me, but he dislikes and barks at my male partner. What can we do?

Answer: The situation is more than just bonding; it is now possession of you at the expense of your partner. Assuming that your partner has not played any part in causing this behaviour, you will need to rapidly socialise your dog to accept him, lest your partner resolve the issue by simply moving on.

Destructive puppy

Our West Highland White Terrier puppy is very destructive regarding toys, books, etc. How can we train him not to do this and how long will it take?

Answer: This is normal behaviour for so young a puppy. Begin by training the members of your household not to leave things lying about thus inviting destruction.

Secondly, divert the interest of the pup to something that can be chewed — a meaty raw bone daily will do the trick. Lastly, your pup is highly energetic and this energy needs to be used up or else he will find his own energy release. A good walk two to three times a day is essential. Terriers tend to settle down between their first and third birthday.

Puppy urinating on owner

We have a two-month-old Jack Russell and a cat. They are lovely together and well toilet trained. However when my husband comes home the Jack Russell urinates all over him. How can we stop this?

Answer: In my experience a dog is never 'water-tight' under nine months of age. The Jack Russell is so excited to see your husband each night that he loses bladder control. Vets are always conscious of this when returning desexed puppies to their owners after surgery! Your dog will gain bladder control by nine months of age.

Adjusting to a second dog

I have a male German Shepherd cross who recently lost his mate, who used to mother him, and he's acting very strangely. We replaced the dog with another one from the RSPCA and we're now finding that he's doing things he's never done in the past. At night he gets confused, and won't sleep in the kennel. What should we do?

Answer: He's getting used to the new dog and feeling a little bit confused and out of sorts. It will take a month or two for them to chum up and form a new arrangement. He is attention-seeking, and if you go and bother about that, he knows he's found out how to get your attention and stay top dog, without having to share with the new dog.

Three dogs

Is it okay to have three dogs?

Answer: As the old saying goes 'three is a crowd'. Do not be surprised if your two resident dogs gang up on the introduced third member. All research shows that animals get on much better in multiples of two. You may not wish to own four dogs as that is quite a pack. Owning three dogs is possible but you will have to go to extraordinary lengths such as wise selection and training to make it work.

Pack rivalry

We have a very gentle Rhodesian Ridgeback bitch, and we've just bought a Ridgeback/Mastiff puppy as a companion. They had been getting on extremely well, but two weeks ago the puppy savaged her, and went through her ear flap and tore her cheek. Since then, it's happened twice more, and I'm sure if we weren't here, he'd kill her. He's been de-sexed, so what do we do?

Answer: They're sorting out a problem of dominance. It's going to be very difficult to stop because it's a natural matter of sorting out who's number one and number two in the pack. You've probably got two dominant dogs and one wants to be the absolute boss and the other one doesn't want to be number two. You can be forgiving for a little while, but if it continues without resolution, the only solution will be to separate the dogs. I am surprised that it is a dog and a bitch fighting. This is normally seen where dogs of the same sex live together.

New dog being bitten by older dog

➥ *Our new Dalmatian, a young male, is being bitten by our older existing female dog. What can we do?*

Answer: There is little doubt that the energetic new dog is being somewhat rough with the older dog in an attempt to get her to play. She is simply putting the young dog in its place. Ultimately they will work things out and they will become firm friends. I would only be concerned if the bites required veterinary attention.

Dog and another pet

➥ *Is it okay to have a guinea pig and a dog together?*

Answer: Of course. But dogs have to be taught to treat other species with respect. All dogs were bred for a purpose and many breeds still have a strong hunting instinct. Dogs suddenly confronted with another type of animal will want to chase it, particularly if the other animal runs away. The chase will result in rough play that often goes too far and injury or death can result. For best results, all puppies need supervised exposure to cats, chickens, ducks, rabbits and guinea pigs (to name a few) from the moment they are brought home.

Pre-owned problems

🦴 *Two months ago we acquired a second family dog, an 18-month-old Beagle, and she gets on very well with every other family member, but she won't come within 20 metres of me. How can I make friends with the dog?*

Answer: There is obviously a learned problem which comes from the previous owner. You've got to be persistent in being nice to the dog, so that it is encouraged to find out you're not what it thinks you are. If you can provide the food, that's terrific, and take it for walks, even if it means someone else has to put on the lead. Similar problems can arise when you take on any pre-owned dog. There will be things about that dog that aren't your fault.

Finding out what your dog is crossed with

🦴 *How can we find out what our dog is crossed with?*

Answer: If your dog is simply a cross between two purebreds a trained eye, such as a vet or experienced dog club officials, will quickly determine what two breeds were involved. For more complex crosses you would need to consider DNA testing, which is not a cheap exercise.

Adopting a dog from the RSPCA

🦴 *I want to adopt a dog from the local RSPCA shelter. How will I know which dog to choose?*

Answer: RSPCA shelters all have trained staff who will interview you so they can establish what your lifestyle is, what expectations you have for pet ownership and what your living conditions are. All dogs available for adoption have been fully prepared — vaccinated, desexed, microchipped, health guaranteed and temperament tested. The staff will introduce you to those dogs whose type and personality best suits you. You can then spend time with the one you choose and almost certainly it will be love at first sight. Best of luck for a very happy outcome.

BEHAVIOUR

Attention-seeking: barking

I'm having trouble with my 11-month-old Jack Russell Terrier who sleeps outside and wakes up very early in the morning. Her barking bothers my neighbours, so I set my alarm for 5.30 and I rush out to the dog, and then she barks at me because she wants to play. What shall I do to stop her barking?

Answer: You're the cause of the problem, because she's got you at the end of the cord. Why don't you put her in the garage to sleep, and lock her up till 7 am, or whenever you want to get up. Stop trying to psychoanalyse her, and be practical!

Digging holes in the lawn

I've got a beautiful and energetic seven-month-old Labrador cross. He's been really well-behaved up till recently when he started digging holes in the lawn. How do I stop him?

Answer: Your dog is bored. He's a very energetic breed. Over the period he was well-behaved he was exploring the back yard, but now he's discovered it all, and to amuse himself he digs holes or pulls washing off the line. He needs plenty of exercise, and I suggest you take him for a two-kilometre walk morning and evening. After the morning walk bring him home and give him a large bone to gnaw on for several hours. You might be lucky enough to convince a retired person to give him a midday walk, which would cut down the distance you have to take him morning and evening.

Separation anxiety: barking

I have a nine-month-old Dachshund and my neighbours are complaining that as soon as I go to work the dog starts barking, and it doesn't stop until I get home at night. What can I do?

Answer: The dog has not been taught to be alone, and to be happy with its own company while you're at work. The dog knows you've left, and as a member of the pack, he wants to know why you haven't taken him with you. He suffers separation anxiety and starts barking to try and find out where you are, hoping you will reply.

The first thing to do is to stop making a fuss of the dog when you leave the house. Don't say anything; simply leave. Arrange with a neighbour or relative to check on the dog during the day and scold it if it's barking. It would help if you could find someone to break the dog's boredom by coming to exercise it during the day. Many retired people would be happy to do that. It will take time and patience to overcome the dog's anxiety, but be persistent, and you'll win. If a neighbour can help you in the process, all the better.

Dog barking when someone is on the roof

➤ *Why does our dog bark when my husband goes on top of the roof?*

Answer: Your dog knows that it is your husband on the roof and cannot understand why he has been left at ground level. His barking is one of happiness and attention-seeking. Perfectly understandable and normal.

Dog jumping fences

➤ *What can we do to stop our Kelpie leaping over a very high fence?*

Answer: Dogs dig out or jump fences due to separation anxiety. Remember that the dog pack does everything together yet in your case the kids have gone to school and you have gone to work leaving one member of the pack behind. Your dog is searching for you. Having said that, make sure that there are no 'stepping stones' such as piles of firewood, bricks or soil up against the fence. Turn the top of your fenceline inwards at about 30 degrees, like a factory fence, by erecting a strip of chicken wire so that your jumping dog hits his nose on the wire. This usually stops the dog escaping, but does not cure the reason for him wanting to get out. Alternatively, why not consider erecting a dog enclosure in your backyard for use when you are not home?

Boss dogs

🦴 *My daughter has a one-year-old Maltese/Shih Tzu cross, and we can't get it to walk on the lead unless it goes where it wants to go. What should we do?*

Answer: It's obviously a boss dog, and it owns you. If the dog's on a choker chain or halter, give a jerk and just keep going. The dog will soon get the message. It would go if I had it on the lead because I'm the boss dog, and the leader of the dog pack, and it would realise, 'If I don't move, something's got to give.' I'm not interested in what the dog is telling me. It will do what I tell it to do. I provide the money for the food, shelter, the comfort and the patting, but they will do what I tell them to do. You've got to take a firm hand. If you don't provide the leadership, the dog is lost, and it doesn't know what to do.

Dangerous dogs

🦴 *A Staffordshire Bull Terrier and a German Shepherd–Dobermann cross live in our area and they've already killed my neighbour's two cats. We reported it to the ranger, and the dogs were sent away for a month, but now they're back again. When the ranger comes around, the owners say the dogs haven't been out, and nothing happens. We're fed up with the dogs terrorising the neighbourhood, so what can we do?*

Answer: Report them to your council. They are the enforcers of the Domestic Animals Act. If there are witnesses that the dogs have been seen killing and mauling, then the council is obliged to do something about it. Write to the chief executive officer of the council and demand that something is done about it. If that does not work write to the State Ombudsman.

If the dogs approach you, stand stock still, and they will lose interest. If you whack them with a stick or call out there will be all sorts of trouble.

New-found aggression in your dog

We recently moved from the city with our four-year-old pure breed Cattle Dog. He seems to have adjusted quite well to the change, but the other day he launched himself at me, as though he was going to bite me. Why has he suddenly become aggressive?

Answer: A male dog at three or four is at the peak of his maleness, and I think that if you get him desexed it will stop most of the dominant behaviour.

Muzzling an aggressive dog

Our Terrier cross loves people but we can't let it off the leash in the park because it is aggressive to other dogs. Can we rely on a muzzle?

Answer: You have only part-socialised your dog. It is okay with humans but not with other dogs. Using a muzzle, which is quite unreliable, is no substitute for lack of good training. First, you must accept the blame for this situation, and then you need to seek the advice of a qualified dog trainer to guide you on a one-to-one basis how to overcome your dog's problem.

PART 5 YOUR DOG PROBLEMS

Disobedient dog

I have a West Highland White Terrier with discharge from the left eye, but she fights like mad to stop me putting the drops in her eye. I take her to obedience training every Sunday, but I still can't hold her down to give her the drops. How do I get her to let me do it?

Answer: The tragedy of situations like this is that owners haven't asserted themselves, and they've allowed their dog to become the boss dog. If you're not the boss dog, you can never achieve anything with the animal, and now you're regretting your decision to let her take charge.

There shouldn't be any necessity to hold her down if the dog has been trained to be number two in the pecking order. Then the dog will do what you want it to do. All dogs, without exception, love to be disciplined, and to follow the leader, who sets the rules and sticks by them. Your difficulty is that you didn't set the rules.

Swap obedience schools, or train yourself.

Voice control

We have a delightful one-year-old Maltese–Bichon Frise cross who is very intelligent and strong-willed, and we've kept in mind your words about boss dogs. Although she tries it on, nine times out of 10 she obeys a powerful voice command. But when we walk her on the beach and she runs free, if she sees another animal or human she just takes off, heedless of our call. We don't want to keep her on the lead all the time, because it's wonderful to see her running off and enjoying herself. How do we deal with this?

Answer: It's part of her defiance mechanism. You haven't got her under complete voice control, and therefore she should be on one of those extension leads which can go up to nine metres. You can't have it both ways: either you put up with her running off, or you put her on a nine-metre lead.

Possessive male dog

🦴 *We have a male Kelpie–Dingo cross and a female Cairn Terrier cross. The male pulls her mattress out of her kennel every few days. Why?*

Answer: The male dog has decided that the mattress is his rightful possession. They say that possession is nine tenths of the law.

Rivalry between two dogs

🦴 *We have two Border Collies. One is a lot older, not desexed and is dominant. If we have him desexed will the younger dog become more assertive? Will castration produce an even playing field?*

Answer: Desexing the older dog will certainly tone down its dominant behaviour although it will not entirely eliminate it. In that sense desexing will create a more even playing field. The younger dog will only become more assertive with the departure of the old dog.

Female dog attacking a male dog

🦴 *We have two dogs which have been together for many years. Now the female is savaging the male. What can we do?*

Answer: Savaging is probably the wrong term as you have not said that the female is wounding the older male and causing trips to the vet. Nonetheless, in this situation damage can happen. The female recognises that the male is aging and at long last she has the chance to become boss. Unfortunately, if the male does not 'give in' the attacks will become more frequent and more intense. If this stage has already been reached the only wise move is to separate the dogs particularly when you are not home. In addition, under no circumstances should you side with the old dog as you will only make matters worse.

Growling at another dog

➤ *We have two male dogs: a Cairn Terrier and a Cocker Spaniel, both desexed. One growls at the other. Will it stop?*

Answer: While I support the ownership of two dogs, I never encourage the purchase of two dogs of the same sex. If both turn out to be dominant dogs fighting will occur to try to establish which is to be the boss dog. Two bitches fighting can be quite vicious. If these growling episodes turn into fighting you may be forced to permanently separate both dogs.

Naughty dog causing damage

➤ *Our dog is naughty and he has been damaging the house we are minding for friends. What can we do?*

Answer: It is not the dog which is naughty. The dog is suffering from separation anxiety and when you are not at home the dog panics and destroys the house looking for you. You have failed to teach the dog that every day members of its human family will be away for some hours, but all will return. You need professional advice as to how to go about correcting this problem. The solution involves a great deal of dedication and work on your part.

Co-existing with cats

I've got a Manchester Terrier, and I'm wondering about how we'd go if we got another cat or kitten, as the terrier used to bail up our old cat, who died 12 months ago?

Answer: Very well. Get a kitten which is extrovert, which you can tell by the way it comes up to you, and how it stands its ground. The kitten will come and possess the house, then you'll let the terrier in, and there will be a slight discussion, and I think the terrier will lose. After that they'll sort themselves out and everything will be fine. I won't accept the comment that dogs and cats can't co-habit. You can make a dog live with anything, providing you set the rules.

Flying with dogs

I have a five-year-old Poodle, and I'm going up to the Sunshine Coast for a two-week holiday. I have the opportunity to take the dog with me, and I'd prefer that to putting him in a kennel, but I'm worried the dog will be frightened by a plane flight. What do you advise?

Answer: A plane flight of two hours is far less stressful on a dog than a car journey of 24 hours to cover the same distance. Dogs are carried in the air-conditioned hold of the aircraft. They're the last thing put on board, after the passengers get on, and they're the first to be removed. It's cheapest to take your dog with you as part of your luggage.

You need to book the dog in at the same time as you book your airline seat, and ask the airline what time you will need to turn up with your dog before your scheduled departure. The airline will provide a suitable carrying cage. There is no need for your dog to be tranquillised. but I suggest it might be handy if you take some Valium to stop yourself worrying!

If you want to check the motels and camping grounds in Australia where you can stay with your dog, contact the motorists' association in your state to see if a booklet is available or do an internet search yourself.

Staying in kennels

We're going away and I'm looking to put my two German Shepherd bitches in boarding kennels for four weeks. We're not going away for the whole month, and I'm wondering if we should go and visit them and walk them while they're there?

Answer: You definitely shouldn't visit them because you will stimulate their desire to go back home with you. Once they're in the kennel they should be ignored by you until you're ready to pick them up. You should not leave them at the kennels for more than four weeks because it can start to affect them. You get mental changes in an animal when the close confinement exceeds four weeks. We won't keep animals at the RSPCA shelter for longer than 36 days.

Taking your dog to work
Is it okay to take our dog to work?

Answer: Dogs are programmed to be members of a pack and to follow the lead of the boss dog. Dogs cannot understand why the human members of the surrogate pack disappear after breakfast and do not return until late in the afternoon. Being left alone all day is the cause of separation anxiety and all of the nuisance problems that drive neighbours bonkers. So if your dog can go to work with you all the better. Check it is okay with the boss and carefully examine the workplace for dog hazards, particularly getting out onto busy roads.

Licking dogs
We have a 12-month-old Bulldog–Jack Russell cross and it obsessively licks people. Why does it do this?

Answer: The dog is enjoying the flavour of the surface deposits on your skin, which is sweat mixed with salt. You're the boss dog, so growl at the dog to tell it to stop. You've got to be tough.

Dog eating cat's droppings
We are babysitting a 12-month-old Shih Tzu and she eats our cat's droppings. Help!

Answer: Disgusting as this behaviour is to you, the pup eats the droppings because of the taste sensation. Placing the cat's litter tray on a platform or in another room where the pup cannot reach it will stop the problem. Eating the cat's droppings will not harm the pup, but make sure both animals are wormed every three months.

Dog eating horse manure

Our dog eats horse manure. How can we stop it?

Answer: Horses eat vegetable matter. Dogs in the wild also eat vegetable matter direct from the stomach contents of a recently killed prey. Revolting as the eating of horse manure may be to you, your dog is enjoying the 'taste sensation'. Have your dog on a strong leash when walking. Allow it to go near horse manure then pull sharply on the leash and scold the dog. Your dog will soon learn of your disapproval and cease the habit.

Inappropriate urinating and defecating

Why do dogs engage in inappropriate urination and defecation?

Answer: Many dog behaviours are there for a purpose when living in the wild but cause difficulty if continued in the domestic situation that we humans have designed for ourselves and demand our pets to conform to from day of purchase. Urine and faeces clearly mark the boundaries of territory for dogs while anal gland secretion individualises each dog. House-training a dog is teaching the dog only to urinate and defecate in an acceptable part of the property and certainly not inside the house. Of course house-training will not stop a dog from marking territory outside of your property, that is why local government has local laws requiring owners to clean up droppings after their dog.

Walking your dog

I have a 22-month-old Kelpie–German Shepherd cross and she has a lovely nature at home, but in the last five months when I walk her on the lead she gets aggressive when other dogs approach me. A lot of people don't walk their dogs on the lead, and when the dogs come up to me I get nervous.

Answer: She should be walked on a choker chain or halter and when she starts to bark or act aggressively, you, the boss dog, should give a good jerk on the lead and growl, 'How dare you behave like that!' That will indicate you won't tolerate such behaviour.

When I walk my dogs I always carry a walking stick, and that's protection for me and the dogs. You've got to be defensive in this life, because there are so many irresponsible people. If you look as though you're equal in power and savagery to the dog which is threatening you, it will back off.

Walking on the lead

I have two big, energetic, well-trained dogs and if they don't get enough exercise they start chewing things at home. My local council has a rule that you must walk the dogs on the lead in the park, but I can't possibly give them enough exercise when they're still on the lead. I don't have enough time to drive them to the one park where the council lets you walk dogs off the lead. My dogs wouldn't attack other dogs so I don't see why they should stay on the lead. What can I do?

Answer: The RSPCA's position is that councils should designate certain parks in each municipality for dogs off leads, but we're not saying it should be every park. You live in a community where you must give a little for the amenity of the whole. If you haven't got time to drive to the off-lead park, then you shouldn't have two dogs. It's sheer arrogance to say, 'I must exercise my dogs, and because I don't have much time I will exercise them where I like.' Every day in my practice I have to treat dogs that have been mauled by dogs that 'never attack other dogs'.

Dogs and the elderly

Should elderly people own pets?

Answer: In my view people living alone, such as the elderly, benefit enormously from pet ownership and if there are little hiccoughs in care it is better to provide assistance than criticism. Contact the Social Welfare Officer in the local municipality, as local government often has helpful schemes to keep older citizens and their pets together.

HEALTH

Bad breath

I have a one-year-old Maltese with very bad breath. His teeth are very good because he eats bones, so I don't think that is the problem. Is it his diet? He's a very fussy feeder, and will only eat raw steak or cooked chicken.

Answer: If a dog has bad breath, the first thing to look at is the teeth and gums. There shouldn't be any problem if he crunches bones. The second thing to look at is diet, which is often the cause of gastric halitosis. Usually halitosis coming from the stomach is worse after eating, then it tails off. The last cause, and the least frequent, is the respiratory system. The problem is probably caused by food, so try the dog on some other foods for a while and see what happens.

Eating bones

I've been told that eating soft canned food all the time can cause teeth and gum problems in dogs. Is that true?

Answer: The Australian Veterinary Association commissioned a study on this and it identified that the continual feeding of soft foods does lead to gum problems. It recommended that this could be prevented if the animal was fed something chewy, like bones, three times a week. The bones should be raw meaty ones. Every time I see gleaming white teeth in a nine-year-old dog I know it's been eating bones all its life.

Bleeding gums

Our dog's gums are bleeding, but it is not due to poisoning. What is the cause?

Answer: As poisoning has been ruled out the bleeding must be caused by a problem within the mouth cavity. First, look at dental health. Decayed teeth or exposed tooth roots are a frequent cause of gum disease and bleeding. Second, look for signs of infection of the lips which may have spread into the mouth cavity. Third, check for tumours of the gums. Lastly, the bleeding may be cause by damage to the mouth by bone chewing or stick catching. Your veterinarian will advise.

Fussy eater

I have two little terriers which are two years old, brother and sister, and the girl has become very fussy in her eating. She loves to stand around me at dinner time and smell what I'm cooking. She turns her nose up at the canned food I put out for her, and ultimately the other dog finishes it off. She likes people's food. We're also finding she's going into the spare room and making puddles, and we're wondering what's causing this.

Answer: She's only food fadding to ensure she gets special treatment from you. When you produce the food for the dogs, put it out for 20 minutes. Either she eats it, or she doesn't. When she doesn't, you remove it, and it is not given to her until the next feeding time, even if it's 24 hours later. Unless you do that, you're going to be controlled by her, at the expense of the other dog, and then you create a whole lot more behavioural problems. The male dog's getting fat because you're allowing the female to get away with food-fadding, and she's too lazy to go out and urinate. She's got you right under control. You've got to be a tougher mother than you are now. Remember, you're the boss dog, not her.

Fleas

⤚ I've been treating my two-year-old Cocker Spaniel for fleas with a rinse once a fortnight, and the dog is still scratching itself to death. What more can I do to get rid of the fleas?

Answer: Fleas don't live on dogs. The reason they get onto dogs is to suck blood on the last day of their life. Sucking blood triggers the release of 1500 eggs, which are usually laid in earth, so you need to check those spots in the back yard where the dog likes to lie, where he may be picking up the fleas. Earth is the main source of fleas, and the second source is bedding and carpet. Fleas will be jumping off the dog onto the carpet.

Watch the dog and discover where it's picking up the fleas. Hose down the soil, fence off the part where the dog likes to lie, or use an insecticidal spray on the area once a week. Wash the dog's bedding once a week in the flea season, and use a can of insecticidal spray to kill fleas and sterilise eggs in the carpet. The carpet will remain free of fleas for nine months.

Once you've controlled the source of the fleas I don't mind which product you use to kill the fleas on the dog. There's no point using a rinse if you can't bath the dog, or if he swims every day, and washes off the rinse. If you can't find the source of the fleas, use a spot-on internal insecticide. Whatever you use, you must follow the manufacturer's instructions.

Skin problems

🦴 *I have two English Cocker Spaniels and for some months now they've had this allergy. They've been scratching, and they have sores, and the hair is coming off their ears. It's mainly on the face and ears, and the skin gets dry and flaky after the sores dry up. I can't figure out what's causing it.*

Answer: The symptoms you describe sounds very much like mange caused by the sarcoptes mite. Fortunately, it is very easy to cure with the right insecticidal treatment. You need veterinary advice to confirm the diagnosis.

Allergy to Wandering Jew creeper

🦴 *Are there any dog breeds which are not allergic to Wandering Jew creeper (*Tradescantia *spp.)?*

Answer: Most dogs are allergic to the milky white sap of the creeper and the usual areas affected are the nose, lips, feet and belly. There are individual dogs which are not allergic, but not particular breeds of dogs.

Licking paws

🦴 *Our Maltese–Shih Tzu–Poodle cross, who is 13 years old, licks his paws. The vet says it is an allergy to grass. What can I do?*

Answer: Always walk your dog on a leash and confine it to a paved footpath. Alternatively, you can buy dog boots for the dog to wear when walking. The aim is to ensure no contact with grass.

Worms

My four-year-old Australian Terrier has been scooting on his bottom lately, and this morning when I took him for a walk I noticed that he passed a creamy-pink worm with his droppings. Should I give him worming tablets?

Answer: What you've seen is a segment from a tapeworm. The dog would have been passing other segments, which irritate him and cause him to scoot on his bottom. Tapeworm cannot be caught directly from another dog, like roundworm. It is usually caught by city dogs eating an infected flea, and the segments commence being passed about 28 days later.

Your dog needs to be wormed with a good quality tapewormer. All adult dogs such as yours need regular worming, particularly against roundworm and tapeworm, every three months.

Hydatids

How can we overcome the problem of hydatids?

Answer: All tapeworms have an intermediate life cycle. A dog which has a hydatid tapeworm will pass eggs and these will be picked up usually by grazing sheep. The cycle is completed when a dog eats sheep meat or offal infected with hydatid cysts. Humans can be an intermediate host with the cysts being found in the chest and abdominal cavities. It is a ghastly disease in humans. You must tackle the hydatid problem through stopping the cycle through dogs. All dogs exposed to sheep — even city dogs visiting the countryside — must be wormed specifically with a tapewormer that kills the hydatid tapeworm, every six weeks throughout the year. Secondly, these same dogs must never be fed sheep meat or offal. Use only canned or dry commercial dog food. Lastly, dogs living in sheep areas must be confined so that they do not chase and kill sheep and eat the abdominal contents.

Epileptic seizures

Our dog has started having epileptic seizures. Why is this happening and what can we do?

Answer: Epileptic seizures can be caused by a genetic defect or an acquired fault in the tissue of the brain. Some conditions of the liver can cause fitting that looks like an epileptic seizure. It is important that you seek veterinary advice, preferably very soon after the dog has had a seizure. Your vet will want to know the history of your dog's condition: when the seizures started; what form they take; the time intervals between seizures; and the time of day that they have occurred, including what the dog was doing in the hours leading up to the seizures. Blood tests will be taken to establish the overall health of your dog. Epilepsy is a word that describes a set of symptoms. *Petit mal* and *Grand mal* describe the intensity of those symptoms. If a diagnosis of epilepsy is made, your vet will guide you on treatment to successfully control the seizures.

Cushing's disease

Our male Cairn Terrier has Cushing's disease. What will treatment do to his quality of life?

Answer: Regrettably, Cairn Terriers are one of a small number of dog breeds that are often afflicted with this condition. Adult to aged dogs are affected, usually caused by a benign tumour of the adrenal gland causing a chronic progressive excess release of naturally occurring cortisone. Once diagnosed, dogs are placed on treatment that will rapidly reverse the symptoms of cortisone poisoning. Frequent follow-up tests will be required to ensure that the treatment dose is correct for your dog. All of this is expensive, but your dog will return to its normal self for the remainder of its life.

Diabetes

We have an 11-year-old Pomeranian diagnosed with diabetes. She has been put onto a special diet but we cannot make her eat it.

Answer: The commercial production of prescription diets over the past 20 years to assist with the treatment of progressive degenerative disease has provided the veterinarian with an excellent tool in the treatment armoury. I suspect your Pom has largely only eaten human food to date and is now rebelling about the new food regime with an entirely different taste. No well dog has ever starved in the presence of food and you must now lay down the law. Provide access to the prescription diet for exactly 20 minutes twice a day. Remove all uneaten food. Expect your dog to refuse this food probably for up to 14 days (yes, you heard correctly!). Once your dog understands that the prescription diet is the only one on offer, it will eat it with relish.

Puffy eyes

My Cocker Spaniel has developed puffy eyes. What is causing this?

Answer: Anything to do with the eyes should be regarded as a medical emergency. Cocker Spaniels are noted for eye and eyelid problems and your dog should be examined and treated without delay.

Back pain

I have a female Labrador who is almost five, and for the past three weeks she's been more subdued, and she yelps when she makes particular movements, or climbs up, or when we touch her in certain places. What is wrong with her?

Answer: She's giving the game away that it's spinal back pain because she is having difficulty getting up. Only a clinical examination will tell you whether it's from the neck area, affecting the whole of the body, or from the lumbar area, affecting the hind quarters.

Heat distress

➤ *I have an eight-year-old Collie–cross who seems to be very distressed with the heat. Should I have his coat clipped to make him more comfortable during the summer?*

Answer: Most of the dogs in Australia were originally bred in the Northern Hemisphere, and they find our heat and humidity hard to cope with because dogs can't sweat — they simply radiate heat. On a hot day you can cool them down by putting the hose on them. The closer the temperature gets to the dog's normal body temperature of 39 °C, the less radiation takes place from the dog, which then becomes hot and bothered.

If you clip the coat, the dog will feel much better, far more energetic, and less distressed by the heat. The bonus is that you renew the coat, and it slowly grows back looking better than before. I clip my terriers three times a year.

Dog leaking urine

➤ *Our three-year-old female, spayed Rhodesian Ridgeback leaks urine. What causes this and can it be fixed?*

Answer: Some desexed dogs, usually female, will develop urinary incontinence characterised by the owner finding a small amount of urine where the dog had been lying, or the coat around the vulva opening being constantly damp. It is important to ensure that no other disease of the urinary tract is involved. Hormone replacement therapy works very well, but other episodes may occur.

Difficulty giving pills to a dog

🦴 *We have an eight-year-old Jack Russell which suffers from seasonal skin allergy. Cortisone is prescribed. He has now developed epilepsy, but refuses to take phenobarbital tablets. What can I do?*

Answer: I am sorry to learn of your dog's problems. It seems your veterinarian is on top of things regarding treatment schedules, so the real problem is the difficulty in you treating your dog. If it is too dangerous to administer the pill to your dog then you need to place the required tablets within a small piece of food that he cannot resist. All puppies should be taught very early in life to accept being examined by their owner, especially the mouth cavity.

Defects in some breeds

🦴 *Are there specific defects in some breeds of dogs?*

Answer: Whenever the gene pool of a dog breed is limited the occurrence of inherited defects rises. Some of these defects are immediately obvious in puppies, but other defects are slow to occur, sometimes not until middle age or older. In June 2009, the Victorian government gazetted a Code of Practice for the Responsible Breeding of Animals with Heritable Defects that Cause Disease, attached to the Prevention of Cruelty to Animals Act. In essence it is now an offence to deliberately breed animals with known inherited defects. Before purchasing a pup always inspect its parents and the rest of the litter. Take someone with you who is an experienced dog person.

Breeding dogs

🦴 *In our area the Council encourages us to desex our pets. We want to breed from our Kelpie dog. What can we do?*

Answer: There are no laws which prevent you owning an entire dog or bitch, but in most areas you will pay an increased registration fee for the privilege. Once you have finished breeding then it is time to have your kelpie spayed for the health and welfare of your bitch.

OLDER DOGS

Back pain

🦴 *We have a 19-year-old Lhasa Apso, and 15 years ago he injured his back, which is still causing some problems. He's blind and deaf, but he's well in himself, and we're frightened to take him to the vet because we might have to confront euthanasia.*

Answer: If the dog is well in himself, you won't be confronting anything because, remember, you own the dog and whether the dog is put down is a matter between you and the vet. It's called informed consent.

Back pain in an elderly dog like this can be caused by two things: degenerative osteoarthritis, or referred pain, from some other condition. If the animal has liver or kidney disease, it will not feel pain there, but in the back. If the dog has osteoarthritis there are new drugs which do not have side effects. Don't give him human drugs for back pain, because they can have dramatic side effects in dogs. You will have to confront the issue of talking to a vet about your dog.

Blindness

Should we put down our old dog because it is blind?

Answer: Certainly not for that condition alone. In the vast majority of cases dogs lose sight slowly and are able to adjust to the condition. I doubt that you recognised the day that your dog became totally blind. Provided that your dog continues to live on the property where it became blind you will notice that the dog will continue to exist happily. Blind dogs are simply not dependent on sight like humans. It is you that will have to change some habits such as only walking the dog on a leash in familiar areas outside of your property.

Elderly person replacing an old dog

My dog is old and, I feel, is dying. I believe I must get another dog, but I am very old myself. What should I do?

Answer: First you must deal with your old dog which you feel is dying. You need veterinary advice as to what is wrong with the dog and what is the prognosis. While I agree with your view that you must get another dog it would be wrong to go ahead without solving the current problem.

Do some homework about choosing a new dog. You need to consider what type of dog you can cope with now that you are much older. Perhaps adopting a middle-aged small dog would be more suitable than starting again with a puppy? Make sure you discuss with your relatives or friends what will happen if in the future you can no longer care for the new dog. If you cannot obtain a commitment from them then I would suggest you join the RSPCA Bequest Program, which will give you peace of mind about your pet's future without you.

DOGS AND CHILDREN

A child's first dog

❧ *What sort of dog should we get first for the children? Is there any difference between genders?*

Answer: A child's first dog is what I regard as a 'learning dog' and as such must be a full-on interactive experience. Regrettably, in my experience the number-one male of the family usually dictates what dog should be purchased, thus destroying the learning dog outcome because he is only considering his needs rather than those of the children. An interactive experience means obtaining a small dog so that the children can learn to pick it up, groom it, attach a leash and walk it, and handle it in many other ways, all under adult supervision. You should get a pup so that the children can experience the changes that occur when it grows up. It should be a sturdy type that can be equally at home outside, inside and in the car. Dog types to consider are small terriers, poodles, spaniels and their crosses. Females have a reputation as homebodies, but there is little difference with a desexed male. Good luck with the family conference!

EMERGENCIES

Bites and stings
Wounds caused by *animal bites* are always infected. Control any bleeding and seek early treatment of the infection.

Bee or wasp stings usually occur to the foot or muzzle. Remove any sting. Anti-histamines will control the extensive swelling reaction.

Bleeding
If a dog is bleeding from the pads, legs, feet, tail or earflaps, don't wash the bleeding area — it makes the bleeding worse.

Wrap a good quantity of cotton wool right around the affected area, not just locally over the wound. Firmly apply pressure to the area by bandaging the cotton wool to the bleeding part using a cotton bandage or sticking plaster.

Once bleeding is controlled, seek treatment. The sooner a wound receives veterinary treatment the better the end result.

Bones caught in the mouth
Check not only the teeth, but between the teeth over the hard palate. Remove any bones using finger pressure or pliers.

Burns

To treat *heat burns*, apply very cold water or an ice pack to the affected area for 10–20 minutes.

To treat *chemical burns*, thoroughly wash the chemical from the affected area using running water. Then seek veterinary treatment.

Burst abscess

Clip hair away from the wound edges and gently bathe away the draining matter with a normal disinfectant solution. Seek treatment for the remaining infection.

Diarrhoea

If diarrhoea continues for longer than 24 hours, seek veterinary advice.

Eye damage

Do not attempt first aid, but seek immediate treatment.

Fits

Control and confine the animal to a quiet darkened place until the fit passes. Do not attempt first aid as the dog may bite you. Seek advice when the fit is over.

Grass seeds

Remove any visible grass seeds from paws. If grass seeds already have penetrated the skin, surgery will be required.

A grass seed in the ear causes the dog to suddenly yelp and hang its head on the affected side. A little paraffin oil in the ear will soothe the pain until the seed is removed.

Motor vehicle accidents

Secure the animal properly. Remember that the animal is confused and in pain, and may bite or scratch you.

Always remove the animal from the roadway and verge. Assess the damage. Visible regular chest movements means the animal is alive. Ask passers-by for assistance or the nearest house to get urgent treatment for the animal.

Poisonings

Don't waste time making the animal vomit. Telephone the vet for advice.

Vomiting

It is normal for dogs to vomit on occasion. Persistent vomiting over 12 hours requires veterinary advice.

If your dog is lost

Don't drive round and round the district. Contact the dog ranger of the municipality, and establish whether he will contact the neighbouring municipalities, or whether you do it.

Alert the neighbourhood network by sticking a notice in the local milk bar, newsagent and butcher, and notify the vets in the immediate area. There is no point in ringing the police as they have no responsibility for dogs.

Once you've done all that, go to the nearest animal shelter, although it usually takes two or three days for the animal to filter through to the pound. It's no good ringing the pound unless the dog is completely distinctive, as your description won't necessarily tally with the description of the receiving person in the pound.

SERVICES FOR YOUR DOG

State Dog Associations
The peak dog association in each state is responsible for the administration of shows and the general running of canine affairs. They register new dogs as pure-bred and provide names and addresses of registered dog breeders. Most keep books and general information on dogs and their care.

AUSTRALIA
The Australian National Kennel Council (ANKC) is the national administrative body for pure breed canine affairs. It does not, however, deal directly with dog exhibitors, breeders or judges. For information concerning breeders, breed clubs or shows please contact the controlling body in your state.
www.ankc.org.au

AUSTRALIAN CAPITAL TERRITORY

DOGS ACT
PO Box 815
Dickson, ACT 2602
Ph: (02) 6241 4404
Fax: (02) 6241 1129
Email: admin@dogsact.org.au
www.dogsact.org.au

NEW SOUTH WALES

DOGS NSW
PO Box 632
St Marys, NSW 1790
Ph: (02) 9834 3022
Fax: (02) 9834 3872
Email: info@dogsnsw.org.au
www.dogsnsw.org.au

NORTHERN TERRITORY

DOGS NT
PO Box 37521
Winellie, NT 0820
Ph: (08) 8984 3570
Email: admin@dogsnt.com.au
www.dogsnt.com.au

QUEENSLAND

DOGS QUEENSLAND
PO Box 495
Fortitude Valley, QLD 4006
Ph: (07) 3252 2661
Fax: (07) 3252 3864
Email: info@dogsqueensland.org.au
www.dogsqueensland.org.au

SOUTH AUSTRALIA

DOGS SA
PO Box 844
Prospect East, SA 5082
Ph: (08) 8349 4797
Email: info@dogssa.com.au
www.dogssa.com.au

TASMANIA

TASMANIAN CANINE ASSOCIATION
PO Box 116
Glenorchy, TAS 7010
Ph: (03) 6272 9443
Fax: (03) 6273 0844
Email: tca@primus.com.au
Website: www.tasdogs.com

VICTORIA

DOGS VICTORIA
Locked Bag K9
Cranbourne, VIC 3977
Ph: (03) 9788 2500
Fax: (03) 9788 2599
Email: office@dogsvictoria.org.au
www.dogsvictoria.org.au

WESTERN AUSTRALIA

DOGS WEST
PO Box 1404
Canning Vale, WA 6970
Ph: (08) 9455 1188
Fax: (08) 9455 1190
Email: k9@dogswest.com
www.dogswest.com

RSPCA ADDRESSES

RSPCA Australia
PO Box 265
Deakin West, ACT 2600
Ph: (02) 6282 8300
Fax: (02) 6282 8311
Email: rspca@rspca.org.au
www.rspca.org.au

RSPCA Australian Capital Territory
PO Box 3082
Weston Creek, ACT 2611
Ph: (02) 6287 8100
Fax: (02) 6288 3184
Email: rspca@rspca-act.org.au
www.rspca-act.org.au

RSPCA New South Wales
PO Box 34
Yagoona, NSW 2199
Ph: (02) 9770 7555
Fax: (02) 9770 7575
Email: mail@rspcansw.org.au
www.rspcansw.org.au

RSPCA Darwin
PO Box 40034
Casuarina, NT 0811
Ph: (08) 8984 3795
Fax: (08) 8984 3635
Email: admin@rspcadarwin.org.au
www.rspcadarwin.org.au

RSPCA Queensland
PO Box 6177
Fairfield Gardens, QLD 4103
Ph: (07) 3426 9999
Fax: (07) 3848 1178
Email: admin@rspcaqld.org.au
www.rspcaqld.org.au

RSPCA South Australia
PO Box 2122
Adelaide, SA 5001
Ph: (08) 8231 6931
Fax: (08) 8231 6201
Email: info@rspcasa.asn.au
www.rspcasa.asn.au

RSPCA Tasmania
PO Box 463
Launceston, TAS 7250
Ph: (03) 6332 8200
Fax: (03) 6332 8299
Email: rspca@rspcatas.org.au
www.rspcatas.org.au

RSPCA Victoria
3 Burwood Hwy
Burwood East, VIC 3151
Ph: (03) 9224 2222
Fax: (03) 9224 2200
Email: rspca@rspcavic.org.au
www.rspcavic.org.au

RSPCA Western Australia
PO Box 3147
Malaga, WA 6945
Ph: (08) 9209 9300
Fax: (08) 9248 3144
Email: rspca@rspcawa.asn.au
www.rspcawa.asn.au

INDEX

Aggression 23, 54, 79–81, 82, 85, 177–8, 196, 198–9
Allergic colitis 70
Allergies 70, 145–6, 209–10
Anthropomorphism 145–6
Australian Companion Animal Council (ACAC) 69, 109, 112
Australian Veterinary Association (AVA) 70, 159–61, 164, 206

Behaviour
 Barking 7, 86–9, 90, 94, 100, 115, 186–7, 192, 193–4
 Biting 61, 92, 174–5, 177–9
 Chewing 61, 71, 98, 187–8
 Defecating 62, 99, 143, 186, 203–4 *see also* Housetraining
 Digging 83, 84, 91, 94, 192–3
 Fetishes 202–4
 Food fadding 78, 207–8
 Growling 84, 92, 179, 199
 Licking 202, 209
 Timidity 59–60
 Urinating 62–3, 99, 139, 186, 188, 203–4 *see also* Housetraining
Boarding 201–2
Boredom 91–2, 93–101, 192–4
Breeders 25, 26–34, 162, 182, 222
Breeding 105–6, 165, 216
Breeds
 Afghan Hound 45–6
 Alaskan Malamute 52–3
 Basenji 46
 Basset Hound 46–7
 Beagle 46–7, 144

INDEX

Bichon Frise 36
Bloodhound 47
Boxer 53
Bulldog 55–6
Bullmastiff 53
Cattle Dog 20, 79, 80, 177, 178
Chihuahua 36–7
Chow Chow 56, 78
Collie
  Border 50
  Rough 50
  Bearded 49–50
Corgi 22, 51, 66, 95
Dachshund 47–8, 144
Dalmatian 56
Dobermann 25, 54–5, 144, 177, 178,
English Setter 44
German Shepherd 25, 51–2, 54, 66, 131, 146, 177, 178
Golden Retriever 44, 66
Gordon Setter 44
Great Dane 56
Greyhound 48
Irish Setter 44
Kelpie 81–2, 83, 92, 105
Labrador 24, 73, 66, 92, 106, 144

Retriever 44, 66, 106, 144
Newfoundland 43
Old English Sheepdog 52
Pekingese 38, 144
Pomeranian 37–8
Poodle 24, 56–7, 95, 218
Pug 38–9
Rhodesian Ridgeback 48
Rottweiler 23, 54–5, 80, 144 177, 178
Samoyed 53
Schnauzer 53
Shih Tzu 56
Spaniel 24, 44–5, 218
  English Springer 45
  Cavalier King Charles 24, 36, 95
  Cocker 45, 95, 213
Terriers 23, 39–40, 146, 188, 214, 219
  Airedale 40, 144
  Australian 144
  Border 40
  Bull 22–3, 40–1, 130, 177, 178
  Cairn 41, 212
  Fox 41–2
  Irish and Scottish 42

INDEX

Jack Russell 42–3
Maltese 24, 37
West Highland 95
Yorkshire 39
Weimaraner 43
Whippet 48, 95

Cancer 146
Cushing's disease 170, 212
Cystitis 139

Dermatitis 65, 127, 145–6
Diabetes 170, 212–3
Diet 67–71, 143, 206, 212–3
Discipline 61, 73, 83–4, 90, 195, 197 *see also* Housetraining, Training
Distemper 66
Dog Act 175, 179–80
Dogs and
  Other dogs 61–2, 102–3, 188–90
  Other animals 190
  Cats 107, 200
  Families 38, 83, 85, 114–5, 178–9, 218

Emergencies 219–221
Euthanasia 170–2

Exercise 71–2, 92, 93, 97, 98–101, 117–9, 116–7, 195, 204–5

Feeding 27, 106, 138, 206, 207–8 *see also* Diet
Free exercise 96–7, 100–1, 116–7, 119–20

Health
  Bladder 139
  Bones 31, 71, 144–5, 213
  Bowel 67, 126, 132, 133, 134, 135, 149
  Brain 66, 140, 221–2
  Ears 65, 126, 141, 209
  Eyes 139, 140, 141–2, 149–50, 213, 220
  Grooming 65–6
  Heart 67, 71, 132–3, 136, 142, 150–1, 170
  Kidneys 71, 139, 150–1, 216
  Liver 66, 71, 140, 211, 216
  Mouth 140, 142–3, 207
  Nose 143
  Reproductive system 143
  Skin 65–66, 126, 130–2, 145–6, 209
  Teeth and gums 70–1, 142–3, 206, 207

INDEX

Treatment 147–52, *see also* Pests, Worms
Upper Respiratory system 140, 143, 206
Vaccinations 27, 66–7, 141
Weight 106, 119, 134, 139, 169–70
Hepatitis 66
Housetraining 62–3, 186, 203–4 *see also* Training, Discipline

Inherited disorders 25, 30–2, 144, 215

Kennel cough 67, 140–1

Leash and collar 59, 72, 86, 116–7, 119, 195, 203

Mating 103–6
Microchipping 27, 181–2, 192

Osteoarthritis 144–5, 148, 216

Pancreatitis 140, 151
Parvovirus 66, 67, 121

Pests
  Fleas 126, 127–9, 208–9
  Mites 126, 130–1
  Ticks 126, 131–2
  Lice 126, 129
  Ear mites 126
  Sarcoptes Mange 125, 130, 209
  Demodex mange 130–1
  see also Signs of illness
Petcare Information and Advisory Service (PIAS) 20–1, 93, 100, 110, 113, 114, 117–9
Pnuemonia 140
Prevention of Cruelty to Animals Act 22, 167, 168, 181, 215
Puppy farms 28, 165–6

Registration 29, 30, 180–2, 216
RSPCA 21, 22, 26, 33, 34, 101, 106, 117, 122, 155, 156, 157, 158–61, 168, 169, 181, 191–2, 202, 205, 218

Separation Anxiety 89–91, 174, 193–4, 199, 202

INDEX

Signs of illness
 Bad breath 142–3, 206
 Coughing 140–1, 142, 150–1
 Depression 138, 140, 151
 Diarrhoea 67, 68, 70, 126, 133, 134, 138, 139, 140, 149, 220
 Lameness 138, 144
 Vomiting 67, 70, 126, 133, 138, 139, 140, 149, 151, 221
Sleeping arrangements 30, 63–4, 107, 192

Tail docking 29, 107, 162–3
Temperament 25, 31, 57–8, 82, 84–6, 106, 192
Training 59–61, 72–3, 83–4, 96, 196, 197–8
 Basic commands 72
 see also Discipline, Housetraining
Travel 200–1

Worms 27, 126, 132–7
 Heartworm 67, 132, 136
 Roundworm 121, 125, 133–4
 Hookworm 121, 134
 Whipworm 121, 134–5
 Tapeworm 125, 135, 210–1
 see also Signs of illness, Treatment

www.ingramcontent.com/pod-product-compliance
Lightning Source LLC
Chambersburg PA
CBHW032336300426
44109CB00041B/1062